D1711677

Gatekeepers
of the
American Dream

(Unaware sentinels are guarding the doorway)

A dissertation about American Slaves, aka "African Americans:" Descendants of American Slaves are suffering through an identity crisis. Lack of internal leadership has caused the American Slave culture to become confused, lost and stagnated. "Uncle Toms," disguised as "African American" leaders, evolved into reactionary "gatekeepers." Inferior leadership is heaping overwhelming devastation upon slave descendants. It demanded this investigation.

By Norris Shelton

Published by American Slaves, Inc.
Louisville, Kentucky

Web site: www.SlavesUSA.com

Copyright © 2010 by Norris Shelton

ISBN: 978-0-976-5417-7-6
Library of Congress Control Number: 2010904275

Book design by Alfred Moreschi
Cover photograph by Alfred Moreschi
Back cover photograph by Marcel Cabrera

Printed in U. S. A.

First printing, May 2010
10 9 8 7 6 5 4 3 2 1

Gatekeepers
of the
American Dream
(Unaware sentinels are guarding the doorway)

By Norris Shelton

This book is written in an effort to shed light on the damage black leaders do to other slave descendants. The author accepts full responsibility for the implications in this document and hopes the reader will understand the necessity of its publication.

While many examples referenced by the author are drawn from the city of Louisville, Kentucky, the University of Louisville and other corporations and businesses in the area, this north central Ohio River city and its distinguished institution of higher learning are merely reflective of the problems spread all across America.

Kentucky's largest city is in the heartland of the United States and is where the author lives, works and interacts with his fellow citizens. This is where he encounters on a daily basis the negative forces and influences he is endeavoring to define, expose and denounce. To this observer, Louisville's political climate, its power structure and its academic environment represent a microcosm of America as a whole. The Louisville community is merely symptomatic and indicative of a national problem. Our country's difficulties are ever-present and all-inclusive.

"Uncle Tom" is a term intended to insult a black person who is perceived by other black people as behaving in a subservient manner to white authority figures, or as seeking ingratiation with whites by way of unnecessary accommodation. Because of ignorance, today's unknowing Uncle Toms do serious damage to their culture without realizing it.

The stereotypic term Uncle Tom comes from the title character of American writer Harriet Beecher Stowe's novel "Uncle Tom's Cabin," written in 1852. Critical and popular views of both the character and the novel have shifted over time, leading to a shift in the term's use. The author does not believe all Uncle Toms set out to intentionally hurt their people but, whether intentionally or unintentionally, he makes it clear that demoralizing damage is still done in an unconscious, systematic way. The Uncle Tom position was actually created by whites out of necessity during slavery. Some slaves stayed in the "big house" and served the master around the clock, carrying out his orders verbatim, not caring how much damage was heaped upon the other slaves because of those orders.

Slaves who worked in the fields despised the master and, for that reason, when they heard the master's children refer to house slaves as Uncle Tom and Aunt Sally affectionately, as if they were relatives, a malignant disgust developed among field hands for house servants. As a result, they started using the term Uncle Tom as a slur. Through osmosis and because Harriet Beecher Stowe's novel, "Uncle Tom's Cabin," was popular, the epithet Uncle Tom has survived and so has the stereotype. Uncle Toms of yesteryear evolved into "African American" leaders of today and are paid a premium to stand guard at the many gates of opportunity. They unknowingly hinder slave descendants from sharing the American dream.

When we study the status of Uncle Tom and the inner workings of the gatekeeper position closely, we see that it was and still is a haven for ignorance and a conduit to transmit perpetual racial subjugation. Uncle Toms were usually chosen because they were proficient in their performance, meek in behavior and illustrated intelligence that could be controlled by whites without fear of retribution. Today, slave descendants who are well-trained often reach Uncle Tom status. Upgraded from house slaves to "African American" leaders, they now stand proudly at the entrances of institutions that are in place to empower slave descendants but, because of imbedded ignorance, they unknowingly prevent the slave culture from entering mainstream American. The word gatekeeper is emerging as a slur term meant to identify modern-day Uncle Toms and expose the harm they do to their followers.

TABLE OF CONTENTS

DEDICATION

History records that, following the American Civil War, four million slaves were freed. In contrast, history gives little account of what became of those slaves. One thing for sure, they didn't evolve into "African Americans" as many people have been led to believe.

On May 15-16, 2009, American Slaves, Inc. held an "Identity Forum" at the University of Louisville campus in Louisville, Kentucky. This education forum was held to properly identify American Slaves and clarify that the offspring of those dark-skinned humans who were captured in Africa, brought to America and then bred to be slaves were and always will be American Slaves.

When the Civil War ended, slaves were released from physical bondage and told they were free. Slaves did not, however, revert back into Africans and reassume an affiliation with their former African motherland because Africa was no longer their homeland because they were no longer Africans. Whites captured Africans, brought them to America and forcefully bred them but, since the offspring were birthed on American soil and indoctrinated with a subservient mind-set by whites and christened "slaves" by America's ruling administration, the progeny were born American Slaves and would henceforth be recognized as American Slaves! The Identity Forum was held to let the public know that slave descendants are being misled. They are not "African Americans." They are in fact Descendants of American Slaves!

Ethnic clarification is necessary if the slave culture is to rise above the listless degradation they inherited from slavery. This book is dedicated to those leaders, black and white, who labor to create a lasting legacy that will emancipate Descendants of American Slaves from racial ignorance.

Having studied the procedure slave masters employed when they were subjugating slaves, we now realize that American Slaves were not only selectively bred physically, they were also maliciously bred mentally causing slave descendants to evolve slowly and ignorant of their earthly birthright. Unaware slave leaders, ashamed of their slave heritage, often allow their group to assume false names without valid reason.

Some slave descendants know their proper identity and understand the seriousness of America's racial situation. They are making every effort to strengthen America by uncovering slavery so the wrong of human bondage can be exposed, explored, understood and subsequently eradicated. Their effort is to repair the damage that was done to American Slaves' mentality by modernizing the way slave descendants think. Though few in number and ill-prepared, these few activists labor with scarce monetary reward, scant recognition and seldom a thank you for their efforts to construct a solid foundation for the American Slave Nation to grow from. To mature and grow strong, weaknesses in the slave culture must be strengthened. Their main weaknesses are lack of racial pride and no leadership to provide proper direction.

Denying their true heritage for such a long period of time, American Slaves have adjusted to denial, depression and misnomers. Unfortunately, false labels have caused their group to wind up stagnated and bogged down with an identity crisis. Since Dr. King was assassinated, leaders have tried unsuccessfully to direct "African Americans" toward freedom not realizing that true African Americans are *born* free! Africans who migrate to America have no connection to slavery whatsoever.

This book is a summary of actions taken by an organization made up of leaders, black and white, who understand slave descendants' correct identity and their true predicament. To seek a cure, they elected to go to the core of the problem which is slavery and the racial ignorance it bred. The president of the organization is a slave descendant who admits to his inherited racial ignorance and early ethnic blindness. He pursued the American dream and, in doing so, he not only realized his proper identity; he found pride in his American Slave heritage.

In spite of encountering numerous obstacles dealing with treacherous

"African American" leaders, he was still able to write this book as a guide for those black leaders who are unknowingly strangling their culture and causing the never ending subjugation of their people. To move the slave culture forward, black leaders must recognize that slave descendants actually exist and agree that American Slaves should be treated the same as other American cultures. Then they must find out why slave descendants are at a standstill and be willing to supply the necessary support that will promote their racial growth and eventual prosperity.

The author's aspiration is to awaken Uncle Toms and let them know it is they who control the future of their people. Some of these leaders have great potential. Hopefully, this treatise will help them see the error of their ways and they will make character adjustments so they can begin collaborating with each other and making intelligent decisions. The following information is untainted. There is no hidden agenda. The author accepts full responsibility for the content of this obligatory work and is optimistic it will help America's racial situation. ❖

God, Please Help Us
(*American Slave mentality ingrained*)

Mr. Charley's prized Uncle Tom

Black leaders are primarily self-anointed. Promoting themselves as "African Americans" (a contrived and misleading designation), they sometimes hold forums expounding on the most outlandish of topics. Their leadership consists of showing off and using big words trying to outtalk each other. Rehashing old news and complaining about the past is not leading; it's merely carnival showmanship. Whoever verbalizes the best by stringing together the biggest words and draws the loudest applause from the crowd is usually declared the winner in such spectacles. Uncle Toms habitually wait for a hot topic to appear in the news or for someone to say or do something that is controversial so they can start ranting about it and draw attention to themselves and thus enhance their hidden agendas. They overreact to what has already happened or parrot what a real leader has already done or said. A genuine leader who has a viable agenda doesn't wait for things to happen — he or she causes things to happen according to his or her plan.

In an effort to help his people, whom he now accurately terms Descendants of American Slaves, the author wrote the book *Crabs in a Barrel,* which deals with Uncle Toms up front, close and personal. Unfortunately, a vast majority of slave descendants don't read, especially books that deal with their racial wellbeing, so the book has yet to produce the sought-after results. Realizing that slave descendants' condition is worsening he also realizes, if progress is to be made, Uncle Toms must be further investigated and openly exposed because descendants of American Slaves' birthright is at stake. Unfortunately, they have no idea what their legacy is; therefore, the author once again takes pen in hand to explain.

Uncle Toms were born into slavery; they survived the Civil War; their progeny masqueraded as leaders during the "Negro" Civil Rights Movement and evolved into today's lowest form of "African American" gatekeepers. In order for slave descendants to overcome racial stagnation so they can move forward, their leaders must understand the necessity of slavery to the building of America, the aftereffect of human bondage and the disadvantage of substandard leadership in a biased, capitalistic society. "African American" leaders avoid talking about the aftereffects of slavery because seemingly no one understands the residue slavery left behind. Eventually, those who claim to be leading slaves descendants must accept the fact that their group inherited a *serious* handicap.

In 1712, Willie Lynch, a slave owner, wrote a convincing letter explaining that he had successfully experimented with mind manipulation and psyche control at his plantation. He had figured out how to control American Slaves' way of existence by installing ignorance into their brains. The process he was advertising consisted of contaminating the slaves' brains with repugnance for their own kind. Repugnance is shame, revulsion and hate, all negative ingredients that are produced by ignorance. Long-lasting ignorance is nurtured by lack of knowledge. The ignorance instilled into American Slaves is similar to a psychosomatic virus that has the capacity to spread rapidly and, encountering no resistance, it multiplies unrestrained. Slave descendants, already inherently ignorant, are naturally oblivious of this creeping virus.

Young slaves were the most impressionable therefore Willie Lynch advocated starting with infants. He assured slave owners that he could turn all American Slaves against each other so they would never pool their resources or join forces and work in synchronization. His main selling point was his bold prediction. He calculated that, in the end, slaves and their descendants would stay alienated and estranged from each other for hundreds of years.

The strongest link in the weakest chain

During slavery, the coveted post of Uncle Tom was a key position and in many cases a lifesaving arrangement for slaves. Some Uncle Toms were instrumental in keeping the whip off a slave's back; some kept slave masters from murdering fellow slaves and, in rare cases, some actually risked their own lives to help other slaves, thus proving their racial worth. The most esteemed among those who sacrificed their lives in support of the slave culture is the Rev. Dr. Martin Luther King, Jr., yet some leaders, including Muslim minister Malcolm X at one point, classified Dr. King as an Uncle Tom.

Unfortunately for the slave culture, any good qualities that Uncle Toms possessed seem to have fallen by the wayside. The negative characteristics, however, carried forward. Somewhere along the way Uncle Tom forgot he was descended from slaves, changed his name to "African American," started mimicking whites and seemingly said to "hell" with helping his people reach true freedom. Yesterday's lowdown Uncle Tom has evolved into today's malicious "gatekeeper." This new breed of Uncle Tom's main job, although unspoken, is to keep slave descendants submerged in ignorance, locked out of commerce, steered away from the economic battlefield and therefore kept from sharing America's wealth.

The author himself was knowingly indoctrinated with a gatekeeper mentality. It seemed to be the only way he could move up in life. After intense training, he became "Mr. Charlie's prized Uncle Tom." Now he's glad he underwent what he terms uncompromising, indoctrination. He didn't fully appreciate it at the time but he was receiving an invaluable education that would be important to his people in the future. Like any true American should, he set out to accumulate wealth, at first, seeking direction from black leaders. After finally realizing they couldn't direct him in this effort, because most didn't understand the basics of business, he started mimicking white leaders because they understood how to make money, and personal wealth was his goal. Once whites showed him how to make money and he saw how easy it was, he wondered why other "Negroes" weren't chasing the American Dream as he was. If behaving like whites and "living large" is what classified blacks as Uncle Toms, so be it. The position of Uncle Tom wasn't all that bad.

According to the growth process, previously restrained intelligence will grow quickly if nurtured properly. Whites, not understanding just how quickly, commented that their new protégé learned how to do business at the higher level at a brisk pace. Even though impressed with his advancement, they were still nonetheless disappointed that his schooling didn't work out the way they thought it would. The Uncle Tom part of the training didn't adhere but the business part he retained and he soon put it into action in the commercial arena in his *own* behalf. Once he reached the status of manufacturer and could see the "playing field" more clearly, he saw how America really works and it didn't look too good for his people. He saw that the slave culture is going through havoc that could turn into unrelenting destruction if something isn't done. But who's to do it? Realizing that no one is held responsible for relieving the pressure that is building in America, especially among slave descendants, he dropped what he was doing and made his way back to the 'hood to see what he could do in his lifetime to improve conditions for his people and therefore for America.

Who best to rectify slavery, a grassroots "alley rat" or a well-known leader?

Necessity is the mother of innovative thinking; need is the motivational force that promotes the thinking process. The need for America to start thinking rationally at this juncture arises because there is a cancerous evil growing in many inner cities across America that demands attention and clear thinking. Since the problem is cultural, no one should be eliminated from the thinking and communication process. Even though communicating problems is what leaders are supposed to do, no one wants to discuss the concern ASI has regarding slavery. When ASI approach "African American" leaders and try to discuss slave descendants' downfall and America's wellbeing, they accuse ASI of whining. They say America is doing just fine and we're just digging in dirt trying to stir up trouble.

One of the unique characteristic of astute leadership is having the ability to look ahead and spot approaching dilemmas *before* they become serious problems. Admitting that a problem exists is the initial step leaders take when they want to head off dilemmas. To correct a problem that is hidden away because a crime was committed and those who committed the crime are in control the victim's destiny but fear retribution, the problem solvers must study both sides of the dilemma so they can understand the opposing viewpoint.

Questions must be answered and positive identification must be made and, since the problem is racial, it must be categorized, labeled, understood by the government and eventually handled by the appropriate authority.

America has never introduced an adequate plan of action that would alleviate ethnic stress, eradicate cultural depression and elevate a depressed group of people.

Cities in America that are having problems are larger cities. Most problems are occuring in predominantly black (aka African American) neighborhoods. That's our first clue: improper identification! Blacks in inner cities are Descendants of American Slaves. American Slaves were a "self-producing" product that was created by corporate America out of necessity. The manufacturing process employed during the creation of American Slaves was slavery. *Slavery was business!* This means the business of slavery is our second clue. Now we must understand the mechanics of the problem so we can perfect a treatment. To comprehend a business as large as the institution of slavery that was illegal and steeped in shame, it's necessary to dissect slavery so we can study the aftereffects of human bondage on humankind and gain a working knowledge of how the slavery business was operated.

Slavery is the cornerstone of American industry. Yet, it has always been considered the most disgusting thing that ever happened in America. This might be true but now that we understand that slavery was simply business, we must lay our emotions aside and deal with the commercial side of slavery with an open mind. Unfortunately, we don't have a lot of concrete evidence. Slave owners and masters, fearing prosecution, destroyed the slavery paper trail. They figured without documentation slavery would eventually just pass away. They figured wrong. It's clear to see that slavery isn't dead, only festering. To prove the point, America interacts with slave descendants, the ongoing product of slavery, on a daily basis. Our intent is to revive the "slave trade" so we can doctor on discrimination from the inside-out and cure the aftereffects of mind tampering at the core. This time around, though, to make sure American Slaves are well represented and gets a fair deal, a Descendant of American Slaves who knows for sure who he is was compelled to became the President of The American Slave Nation. His duties are to manage the slave corporation and direct the newly bred slave culture.

America is an industrial giant and slavery will always be a vital part of America's foundation. For America to stay strong and grow even stronger, we must strengthen American Slaves. If not, the foundation of America will continue to grow weaker until it starts to deteriorate and then crumble. That's why a peaceful revolution must be carried out in America before ignorant leadership allows America's simmering situation to detonate without clear warning. The warning signs are actually popping up everywhere but, because slave descendants are improperly identified, leaders don't associate inner-city problems and "African American" disarray with slavery.

Like any explosive situation that wasn't terminated properly, the fuse of slavery has been smoldering and, without warning, it could still blow up in our faces. Because of racial ignorance and hypocrisy, America has become overly vulnerable on too many fronts. We can ill afford to have a violent reaction from slavery, lest it rupture the foundation of our nation.

ASI has never started a revolution before, but there couldn't be that much difference between starting a *peaceful* revolution than turning a business around that is on the decline. It's really the same thing. Having counseled scores of business owners and started many corporations of various denominations, ASI's president has been well-trained for the job ahead (read *Crabs In a Barrel*). ASI will simply use the same formula to jump-start slavery and breathe life into the American Slave Movement that ASI's president used to start businesses and counsel businesspersons whose businesses were not profitable.

Profitability is our goal

Before we get underway, it's essential that we understand the variables of the business that is to be revived and also the product that was once produced by the business. We will begin by understanding American Slaves and the dire predicament they find themselves in: Slave descendants are a largely confused people, and the author should know. For decades, he studied America's racial situation trying to figure a way to help his culture rise above racial confusion and disorder. He found that the main reason why slave descendants are suffering is their leaders haven't been awakened. They are still asleep from slavery, submerged in an Uncle Tom like coma and their followers are floundering helplessly. When the Civil War ended, slaves weren't given any instructions that would show them how to blend in with the dominant white culture.

Instead of being properly freed from servitude, slaves were evicted from slavery while submerged in ignorance, poverty-stricken and had no means of survival. Attempting to prosper in a chauvinistic, industrial society without knowledge is a mammoth handicap that cannot be overcome unless first recognized, pointed out and ultimately understood; then it can be reversed and turned into intelligence that can overpower entrenched bias so wealth can be accumulated.

America has never introduced an adequate plan of action that would alleviate slave descendants' ethnic stress, eradicate their cultural depression nor elevate this depressed group. The school system has never initiated a special education program that would enlighten a people who are *racially* ignorant. These two scenarios paint a dismal picture but it gets worse. Leaders, black and white, are so confused they don't even know where to start looking for answers! They keep trying to improve the deteriorating conditions of "African Americans" and that's America's predicament in a nutshell! Leaders simply don't understand the problem or even who's having a problem.

In a state of confusion, white leaders, thinking it's a black problem have backed away from the predicament. "African American" leaders, overly skeptical of constructive criticism, usually attack any suggestions that could lead to change. Not understanding the problem or that the author's intention is to help them do their jobs, "African American" leaders rebuke him when he maintains that they are *not* "African Americans" but more accurately Descendants of American Slaves. American Slaves are more American than any group of people in America. That's why slave descendants' proper identity is so vital to the future well-being of America.

America needed people to do manual labor, so white Americans bred slaves. It was necessary that the slaves be dark-skinned so they could be distinguished from whites, so whites captured dark-skinned Africans to be the initial breeders of American Slaves. Racial bias has always been firmly in place in America and, so far, there is no plan to counterbalance neither the current effect nor the lingering aftereffect. Those in a position to provide proper aid to slave descendants, not understanding the problem or who's having a problem, continuously dispense aide to the wrong people: Commercial aid is dispensed to the general public by way of minority programs, and welfare is awarded to anyone who says they are needy. Providers, listen up! It's the American Slave culture that need and deserve help — not individual "African Americans!"

To solve a problem that is ingrained, the problem solvers must understand the composition of the problem, why, when, where and how it started and the aftereffect of neglecting the problem. Clearly, Descendants of American Slaves' problem started in America and it will certainly end in America — not in Africa! To straighten out

America's racial misunderstanding and stop slave descendants from self-destructing, we'd better first know who we are trying to straighten out and what it will take to get the job done. Different cultures have different needs. The needs of slave descendants are not the same as those of Chinese Americans, Mexican American and *definitely* not African Americans. These are immigrant cultures. America's racial problem in regard to slave descendants is the aftereffects of slavery. Immigrant cultures have no connection to slavery whatsoever! Slave masters didn't design immigrants' mind-sets, and immigrant cultures weren't abandoned in America at the conclusion of slavery and Civil War. Foreigners come to America, some legally and others illegally, through the United States Immigration Service for different reasons but mostly to gather wealth and seek a better life.

When the term "African American" is used to identify slave descendants, it does serious damage to the slave culture because it inaccurately identifies a downtrodden group of people and stops them from getting the help they rightfully deserve. The term "African American" is legal terminology used by the Immigration Service to classify immigrants from African when they migrate to America.

Before immigrants can become citizens, it's a requirement that they understand America and American commerce. They are made aware of how to advance *economically* so they can support themselves and not be a burden on the American economy. Although slaves were bred in America for commercial purposes, American Slaves never received any commercial guidance. As a result, they have no concept of how *commercial* America really works. Since slaves have never been able to rely on their group for financial support, they have drifted toward relying on welfare and minority programs to exist.

Slave leaders must learn the significance of slavery to the building of commercial America and the legalities that surround the enslavement of their foreparents. They must understand that the importance of slavery hasn't dwindled — *it's downplayed because of its importance!*

Immigrants understand America; slave descendants don't. Immigrant knowledge opposed to slaves' ignorance allows immigrants to supersede the slave culture in all advancement categories.

Leaders, white and black, are looking everywhere for answers to inner-city problems; overlooking that inner-city neighborhoods are predominantly black. Black Americans are Descendants of American Slaves! To cure a *racial* problem go to the core of the problem. Leaders must revisit slavery so they can understand what and who they are dealing with and what went wrong! The first thing they will see is that the slave culture has never been structured. American Slaves need and deserve a racial advancement plan that will assemble their culture properly and show slave descendants how to prosper; not as individuals, but as a unit. A plan that would organize the slave culture, control and secure the future existence of slave descendants should have been drawn up before the Civil War even started *and most certainly* when it concluded.

The author finally recognized the abuse his group is experiencing. He not only endured racial discrimination, personally; he studied it carefully. The blundering disparity and blind abuse he went through when he was trying to advance in business wasn't caused by whites but by those he thought were his ethnic leaders. They were trying to act like whites, which is not a bad thing; except they were acting like bigoted, non-caring, lowdown, *slave-hating* whites! In the industrial arena, he not only found out how America operates, he finally understood why slaves act like "crabs in a barrel." Dealing with faulty leadership helped him understand his people and also their plight.

As an elder, he's lived long enough to look back and see the broader picture. He has been called "colored," "Negro" *and* "African American," only to find out he was a slave descendant all the time — and that was the problem all along! Now that he understands what is ailing his people, he has accepted the responsibility for issuing a plea for slavery to be properly rectified by way of fair play and litigation: thus his calling.

American Slave, revolution?

"African American" leaders are clearly misrepresenting Descendants of American Slaves. Some "African American" leaders are spreading the notion to slave descendant children that there is no such distinction as Descendants of American Slaves, anymore. They say we're all Americans now and discrimination is *against the law.* Quite the contrary; that's the same kind of garbage slave masters used to feed young slaves during slavery: "Tell the ignorant "darkies" anything. They have no other choice but to believe it because they have no other source of information." Descendants of American Slaves do exist and are *openly* discriminated against in their own country — *even by the law!* — And it's clearly because of who they are! The slave culture is trapped at the "bottom of the barrel" in all equality categories. This discrepancy is caused by discrimination solely because the slave culture has an identity crisis and, because of ignorance, their heritage wound up being poverty.

America is a *legalized* society that is fueled by commerce and controlled by paperwork and accurate documentation. This means inappropriate designations are not legal, recognized or authorized. To move the slave culture forward in a paperwork society that recognizes accuracy, it's foolish for people who are so distinctly identifiable to try to pretend to be another ethnic group. Impersonating another culture only serve to confuse authorities and slow down the advancement process. Descendants of American Slave mimicking immigrants' keeps leaders, black and white, befuddled and the bulk of slave descendants always at square one. America is moving forward at breakneck speed and slave descendants are easing backwards. This explains why the racial disparity gap between whites and blacks is widening at a quickened yet seemingly unnoticed pace.

When slave descendants' racial advancement, or lack thereof, is compared to other cultures that have immigrated to America since slaves were misled into believing they were free, we see that the slave population is stagnant *mainly* because the average black leader who *claims* astuteness is submerged in racial unawareness. Inadequate communication between the black and white cultures is why this blatant ignorance is allowed to run rampant across America.

Everyone knows the truth about slavery but is wary of telling the whole story, which should be obvious: Slaves were bred in America. During the breeding season, which took *many* generations, the living form that became American Slaves was forced to mate with whomever slave masters and owners chose, including slave masters and owners. Slave masters selected breeding partners based on the owner's whims and his profitability expectations. Therefore, the people who are descended from American Slaves, some dark-skinned and now because of "race-mixing," some light-skinned, are Descendants of American Slaves — not "African Americans!" If we Americans are serious about strengthening America and if we really want to improve race relations in our country, we must focus on cultural details and take a closer look at slavery and the enduring aftereffects it left behind.

When Dr. King was alive, many "Negroes" followed him. If they had followed his direction after he was assassinated, slave descendants likely would have wound up exactly where he told all Negroes to go: to the "economic battlefield." Luckily, the author followed his direction. Now that he understands what Dr. King was trying to tell his followers and seemingly "African American" leaders don't, he feels duty bound to pass on to his people what information he gathered while in business.

To succeed in a business-driven climate like America, slave descendants must understand the effects of economics in a society that boasts freedom but champions discrimination. Most slave descendants who claim to be leaders don't understand economics in a society where racial bias is the norm. To move forward in a biased commercial setting that claims fairness, careful planning in regard to *ethnicity* is a must every step of the way. Thus far, "African American" leaders refuse to discuss their ethnicity and racial wellbeing intelligently, even among themselves. They have no plan at all that will advance their depressed followers; they don't even know they need one. Still they resist the methodology the author brings to the table.

When confused racial leaders reject constructive directions, knowing they have no plan that will help their people advance, they're *knowingly* blocking their own peoples' progress! Having no other recourse, the author is obligated to blow the whistle on gatekeepers, their positions and also gatekeeper institutions.

Because of the harm Uncle Toms do to their followers, who are clearly innocent, exposing gatekeepers is an obligation that all Americans inherited — *and it's purely business* — not personal! It is the inherited duty of *all* slave descendants who understand business to help their people excel in a business driven environment. The effort American Slaves, Inc. expends exposing gatekeepers is not intended to be mean-spirited or disrespectful. It just so happens that gatekeepers are blocking the only feasible pathway slave descendants can take into mainstream America. Taking them head-on is the only way we at ASI know how to get our point across and move *grassroots* slave descendants past obstinate gatekeeper barriers. The president of ASI has asked confused leaders many times to give him direction or either move out of his way. He has told them: "If I'm wrong and slave descendants truly are "African Americans," tell me so — debate me! It's your duty to make me understand! If I'm right and they are not "African Americans," it's your duty to help me lead our people out of this hopeless degradation! Either lead follow or get the 'hell' out of the way!"

Why wouldn't "African American" leaders want to help ASI if they know we're doing our *very* best trying to help an abused people? When we ask existing leaders for help, many just look at us with confused looks on their faces and keep standing in the way of slave descendants' cultural progress. What are we to do with these people who won't do their jobs, keep living under their tyranny, abiding by their rules and accepting unnecessary abuse without saying anything — because they are high-and-mighty — seemingly untouchable — *and that's the way it's always been?*

Getting down to the real "nitty-gritty"

No matter what slaves have been called — colored, Negro, black and now "African Americans" — the slave culture was born and bred right here in the United States of America. That's an *obvious* fact that has *huge* ramifications. It signifies that American Slaves are the only *natural-born* offspring of America and a clear representation of America's "melting pot." Unfortunately, their leaders, unaware of their racial being, are cravenly submissive and don't have the courage to confront whites and claim their true birthright. Could it be they don't know who slave descendants are? Well, for starters, the slaves' culture is a unique group of citizens that was bred by America's dominant white culture. Because of their innocence and inexperience, slave descendants are expressive, have various hues, different grades of hair, talk with a slavery accent and use slang. These differing characteristics are inherent. Slave descendants are a surviving subculture that was bred in bondage and intended to be controlled by fear, ignorance, shame and violence perpetually. Classified as mere animals and considered in no way human, slaves had no say in their lives; that's why ASI says American Slaves are innocent.

A group of human beings that are thoroughly brainwashed, maliciously indoctrinated with a slave mentality and the essence of their being systematically injected with the blood of many nations against their will, have no other choice but to evolve multihued and confused. A group of people who have been abused and then abandoned in ignorance will develop into an angry bemused populace who are lost and exasperated. This tells us that negative, self-defeating components went into American Slaves' composition. The disarray we see in black neighborhoods is the aftereffects of slavery surfacing in the midst of a leaderless people.

At the conclusion of corporal slavery, to make sure American Slaves' state of mind remained in a subservient mode, the only stewardship available to them were trained Uncle Toms who retained their leadership status who had been programmed to be totally ineffective.

Humans that are born and bred to be slaves will evolve ashamed of their existence and have no hope for the future. If these same human beings are christened slaves, given an entirely new mind-set, trained to be slaves, live abusive lives of slaves and then are abandoned in ignorance, their offspring will evolve into what — African Americans? Not likely! It's important that American leaders realize this very important point. Slave masters didn't set out to create "African Americans." They set out to breed slaves. Their prime objective was to create a dark-skinned subculture they could control indefinitely! History confirms that's *exactly* what they created, and whites are still in control! During slavery, slaves were the most valuable commodity produced by America. Slave masters had no intentions of *ever* shutting down the lucrative industry of slavery or losing control of American Slaves. It took an act of war to force slave masters and owners to stop breeding slaves and bring *corporal* slavery to a violent, bloody halt. Unfortunately, the bloody halt didn't include closure. The wound was deep — all the way to America's core — and it was left to fester.

The North won the Civil War and American Slaves survived but, in the end, white Americans, for obvious reasons, preferred to erase the dark chapter of slavery from this nation's existence. Slave descendants, frightened, ashamed and not knowing any better, gladly concurred and voluntarily helped whites sweep slavery under the rug. Not caring whether American Slaves suffered, survived or died, America just "pulled-the-plug" and turned her back on her only conceived offspring.

There was no legislation passed that would force slave masters, slave owners and those who benefited from slavery to rectify the aftermath of human bondage and mind-manipulation. American Slaves had just undergone *decades* of breeding which included depraved mental programming and extreme physical servitude. The defective mental transformation slaves received was designed to spread unimpeded — and the North had knowledge of this evil plot! Yet, when the Civil War was over, America allowed the guilty to just walk away. Failing to construct a follow-up plan, American leaders left a confusing mess to fester in plain sight but, because of the callous leadership that evolved, it is still cruelly disregarded.

Excessive greed: the purest form of ignorance

Using hindsight to better understand slave descendants' plight, it's doubtful that slave masters realized they were bringing another race of people into existence when they were breeding slaves. They probably never considered that someday slavery would have to be dealt with. Most likely, they just saw a straightforward, cost-effective way to make huge sums of money and *someday* would just have to take care of itself. So what does this tell us? Well, on the one hand, it tells us that, even though hardhearted and uncaring, early American whites were quite savvy. Like cultures before them throughout history, they played God and successfully created a human subculture. Conversely, though, they took no measures to straighten out the mess they created, nor did they make an attempt to cultivat the culture they bred. Therefore, they are proving they are the "devil's henchmen."

White Americans of today are showing *unbridled* ignorance by not recognizing that the ethnic group their foreparents created should be upgraded and treated equal to other American subcultures. This leaves those of us who have gained a small amount of intelligence to suspect there is still a lot about slavery yet to be uncovered. For instance, why does the slave culture, *born and bred right here in America,* lag so far behind other cultures that have come into America since slavery? There could be many reasons; some we will explore in later chapters but one reason is already known — gatekeepers — white and black! They have a tradition of morally discrediting slave descendants.

Gatekeepers use the news media to spread carefully prepared propaganda that carries negative depictions of slaves; except they use the expression "African Americans." That way slave descendants, already ignorant of their identity, don't know they are being talked about behind their back. The information-highway and other technologies have silently branded slave descendants as a *criminal* subculture, which is not true. History teaches that, in order to create a safe haven for slave owners, a docile mind-set was necessary; therefore, slave masters bred slaves to be frightened, meek, honest and loving.

After so much negativity, many slave descendants took the cue and started projecting a negative image back to America. Now, seemingly everyone is wondering what is wrong with the inner-city people; overlooking that the slave subculture has always been *economically* deprived and, since Dr. King's demise, they have been without internal leadership. With no leader who had their best interest at heart to tell them what to do to better themselves, many slaves had no other choice but to take their cue from what society projected: lower their moral standards and become criminals to survive. When slave descendants have leaders with the guts to tell them to act differently, they will act differently. It's a leader's job to lead his people. If leaders don't know how to lead a group of people, it's their job to gain advancement knowledge and leadership skills. If it is found, however, that they are not mentally equipped to lead groups, or don't have leadership capabilities, they must learn how to follow!

ASI believes the leaders of each American culture have a responsibility to make sure their nationality lives up to the high standards that America boasts. Therefore, this document is aimed primarily at "African American" leaders but, when all is said and done, the buck always has to stop at the top. Whites have an obligation to take the lead in straightening slavery out. After all, they worked hard to create this mess. It's their job to tell slave descendants who they are and how to merge into mainstream America. But, on the other hand, slave descendants can ill afford to wait for whites to come to their rescue because the first step whites would have to take to help upgrade the slave culture is to positively identify the people. Most whites don't have the stomach to classify the slave culture by calling so-called "African Americans" Descendants of American Slaves in public.

Because of the shame of slavery, fear of reprisal and bigoted hate which adds up to ignorance, the whole story surrounding slavery is being covered up. Whites fear slave descendants waking up from slavery and becoming aware of just how much damage their foreparents did to the slave culture. They assume because of simmering hate, violence would surely erupt. Whites' hidden shame for the atrocious actions of their foreparents and fear of repercussion from slave descendants, unless overcome, dictates that the slave culture will remain in a retarded, ignorant state indefinitely or until it's too late for recovery, which is what slave masters were betting on.

It's devastating to American Slaves to keep evolving without proper nurturing from the dominant culture that bred their ethnic group. The chance of violence erupting is zero if the rectification of slavery is led by leaders who have read and understand *America's Little Black Book*. It explains that slavery was necessary to the building of America. It gives details in simple language how to rectify slavery in an upbeat, peaceful manner. That's the whole idea behind rectifying slavery at this early stage: Head off violence before it happens! That's why ASI has been working diligently to come up with a feasible plan that will head off *even* the threat of violence from a people who are ashamed of their being and know they are still being mistreated. They just don't understand the mistreatment, and that's the danger. Here's a plainer picture: Imagine ignorant slaves growing up wild in the midst of a white controlled environment, licking their wounds and harboring hate for the white controlled establishment for hundreds of years because they know what whites did to their people. That's a potentially volatile situation — the perfect ingredients for disaster!

ASI has conferred with white leaders on this issue. Most would like to help but some feel it's probably too late for the "sleeping giant" to wake up, smell the coffee and get all "worked up." This attitude suggests that slave descendants are beyong help. Some whites figure like slave masters did at the conclusion of slavery: Destroy the slavery paper trail, cover slavery up and genocide will happen automatically. It won't! Simply, because it's against America's principles and it weakens the foundation of our nation. ASI warns that Americans shouldn't bury their heads in the sand on the issue of slavery. It's dangerous to overlook simmering situations that are volatile and unstable. ASI's effort is to come up with a solution that will remove the threat of rectifying slavery and, at the same time, create a positive situation for all Americans.

No Revolution — An American Slave Movement

The responsibility of nurturing the newborn falls to the creator of the newborn. The same ruling would obviously apply to the breeders of a newborn culture. Realizing that America's racial situation could worsen on short notice or get out of hand altogether, ASI set our course to fig-uring out ways to get whites directly involved *up front* in helping take the threat out of litigating slavery. Whites have proven to be a terribly belligerent people when they feel threatened. They not only have the stubbornness to keep the slave culture on its knees indefinitely, they also have the resources to create an even bigger mess than they've already created and, if things were to get out of hand, they are not above accus-ing American Slaves of starting the trouble so whites won't have to bear any of the blame. If this should wind up being the case, Descendants of American Slaves would surely wind up bearing the blame *and the shame* for white's atrocities, as they are currently doing and then being wrongly punished instead of whites, as is currently happening. Whites would spend hundreds more years feeling good about the great America they built and slavery would remain covered up. The suffering of American Slaves would continue but, because of ignorance, racial abuse would re-main unrecognized waiting for the next untimely eruption.

It is well-established that there is a huge cultural difference between whites and blacks. What we have been overlooking is that there is an even larger cultural gap between "African American" gatekeepers and grass-roots slave descendants. When black people refer to "uppity Negroes" as Uncle Toms, it is assumed this is just spiteful ranting and name calling that no longer holds meaning. It wasn't until after ASI sponsored a two-day summit at the University of Louisville that the term Uncle Tom in regard to racial indignation was clearly understood.

The U of L summit was held to focus on *America's Little Black Book,* the book that clarifies why slave descendants have wound up being sec-ond-class citizens in the country where they were bred. It also explains that the slave culture has evolved slowly because whites who bred this group of people bred them to be animals, not humans! American Slaves' sole purpose for being on earth was to labor and serve the dominant white culture. Since slaves were considered merchandise, every white person, even those who couldn't afford the price of a slave, could still control slaves and abuse them at will just as they could a mule or any defenseless animal. *America's Little Black Book* further explains that, following the Civil War, whites abandoned American Slaves and left the slave culture standing on the side of the road without giving them further instructions and slaves haven't advanced beyond that point. Instead of going forward, slave descendants are still stranded on the side of the road, lost and confused, waiting for someone to tell them what to do and which way to go.

When American Slaves were ejected from slavery *as a group* they automatically became an American sub-culture. Unfortunately, the whites who fought so hard to free American Slaves overlooked that, when slaves were freed, they were juvenile, inexperienced and still ignorant. They had no direction, options or resources. Their freedom consisted of being expelled from slavery and shoved headlong into an inhospitable business environment that hated them and left there to suffer indefinitely. This tells us that slaves weren't freed. They were forced into disaster — a huge difference! The underlying disgust slave descendants feel for whites today developed because whites bred and enslaved their foreparents and, after the Civil War ended, they abandoned them without any means of survival. When we take into consideration the evil actions of whites during slavery, their brutality during the "Negro" Civil Rights Movement and their lack of concern today, we can understand why slave descendants harbor ill feelings towards whites. Unfortunately, because of these ill feelings, a serious misconception has developed. Black Americans, submerged in confusion, are misreading America's true racial situation. It allows gatekeepers to flourish and gatekeeping institutions to exist.

What this means is slave descendants are still being taught unconsciously and *sometimes* consciously that evil whites are to blame for the condition their people are in today. There is truth in that rationalization because whites bred the slave culture, abused them and then ran off and left them behind in misery. However, this notion is also misleading and can be a gatekeeper tactic that allows Uncle Toms immunity from righteous attack and a shield to hide behind.

Granted, it was whites who raped the slave culture into this racial mess but evolution took place and things changed. It is not necessarily whites of today who are blocking slave descendants' way out of this cultural chaos. In great part, it's "African American" leaders! Once they progress into a gatekeeper position, they block slave descendants from advancing into mainstream America. Unwilling to shoulder their share of the blame for their cultures' downfall, weak leaders start harping about what happened to "African Americans" in the past and point the finger of guilt at whites. Since slave descendants don't know any better, useless leaders shift the blame for their group's sluggishness to the white culture instead of admitting that they simply don't know what they are doing.

Whites show their ignorance when they keep funding the same black organizations year after year that are supposed to represent slave descendants. Whites are bound to know these organizations aren't producing any favorable results, even if blacks don't. "African American" leaders don't have the mental acumen

American Slaves' sole purpose for being on earth was to labor and serve the dominant white culture. Since slaves were considered merchandise, every white person, even those who couldn't afford the price of a slave, could still control slaves and abuse them at will just as they could a mule or any defenseless animal.

to understand America's true racial situation. Cursed with tunnel-vision, they are so far-removed from the reality of their own situation until there is no way they could see the entire playing field clear enough to gain an accurate analysis of America's true racial state. When fortune smiled their way, "African Americans" leaders left the 'hood and started associating with upper-crust whites. As time passed, some of them eventually acquired the ability to look back and understand what was happening to their people. Unfortunately, it was too late. Greed had already set in and they were comfortable. Now they're frightened and fear if they were to tell the American public *exactly* what slave descendants' racial situation truly is, comparatively, they would be putting their own comfort zone in jeopardy and might have to forfeit their gatekeeper rights.

Whites have always misled Uncle Toms and, unfortunately, Uncle Toms have always refused to accept leadership from their own kind. As a result, gatekeepers aren't able to summon the courage that comes from cultural unity to overcome their racial fear. False pride stops them from seeking advice from within. Without recommendations from grassroots slaves, they have no way of obtaining firsthand information from the source of the problem. Without this vital data, they will never know what to do about the slave culture falling apart at the seams. When racial incidents erupt, "African American" leaders usually try to act like whites: They blame innocent slaves for the eruption. Conversely, though, if there is money involved, they first cash in on the flare-up; then they bury their heads in the sand and pretend racial chaos isn't happening and ride out the storm. It's customary to berate those slaves who are being abused.

Leaders, white and black, must take their heads out of the sand. Racial discrimination has to be talked about and it must be tackled head-on. That's where ASI comes in. American Slaves, Inc. welcomes the opportunity to represent the only offspring of the richest, most powerful country in the world, even if they do appear to be turning wild; they just need direction. "African American" leaders had the chance to represent slave descendants but, thinking slaves are beyond help, they were ashamed to be identified helping the helpless, so they passed up the opportunity. Now, shame won't allow gatekeepers to say they have been wrong, which is a *huge* mistake — *we have all been wrong!* Admitting facts shows signs of intelligence. ASI is not ashamed to say that the slave culture is in utter turmoil because now we know what to do about it, and we're doing it. Nevertheless, as we move forward, things could still get ugly from *within*. Lowly slave descendants have a problem when they hear the truth about who they are. Especially since they have been living in shame, believing an "African American" lie, and so-called "African American" leaders won't admit they were wrong.

In this day and time and according to the people's needs, "African American" leaders and the splinter groups they represent are *clearly* outdated, totally inadequate and don't belong in the positions they are in. Slave leaders see corporate mergers taking place all over America and the world, yet black leaders don't realize that merger within their group is *absolutely* necessary if the slave culture, *a product of corporate America,* is to survive in a corporate setting. "A house divided against itself cannot stand!" For slave descendants to stand together, slave leaders must rely on the core of their being for support, which is slavery. It is the only common denominator strong enough to merge slave descendants together so they can stand as one!

"African American" leaders must compare the slave culture to other American nationalities so they can see what the differences are. Then they must figure out solutions to spanning whatever gaps they find. Many slave descendants have achieved PhD status, but few of them are taught to think properly in regard to their culture. In fact, because America boasts being an impartial society, slave descendants are unconsciously taught that it's discriminatory and shows bigotry on their part if they show partiality by helping their culture more than they help other American cultures.

There is no institution in America where slaves who are in a position to help their people can go and render aide *directly* to their own kind except at American Slaves, Inc.

Welfare reform

Nature and America both teach us that parents have an obligation to their offspring. Therefore, America has an obligation to the slave culture just as any parent would to its child, and it doesn't matter whether the offspring is born out of wedlock or within the bonds of holy matrimony. Until the child can fend for itself, whoever fathered and bore the offspring bears the responsibility of rearing the child. Hopefully

"African American" leaders will understand the ramifications of such an *important* statement. Narrow-minded bigots will jump to the conclusion that slave descendants are seeking a handout. Leaders who are astute would be insulted at the very notion — we're talking business here — not seeking welfare!

It's unfortunate that a large majority of slave descendants have *unconsciously* regressed to sitting around waiting for welfare checks. Welfare is a hindrance in a commercial society. In some cases, however, welfare is direly needed but, on the other hand, if assistance is unwarranted but still sought and then accepted, it gnaws away at character.

When welfare and other honest assistance are intentionally abused, they usually become habit-forming. Regrettably at this point, yes, handouts are necessary and *vital* to the slave culture. Too many strong black males (potential breadwinners) are behind prison walls and a majority of those who aren't can't find gainful employment. Black women had no other choice but to take over black households and endeavor to fend for their families because black men, having fallen prey to a discriminatory society, have wound up being the last to be hired. The female species, inherently prone to being cared for and black men unemployed or either incarcerated is the reason why welfare is so widely accepted and has become the norm in the slave culture.

Another reason why welfare became popular and acceptable is because a large percentage of slave descendants have lost the respect they once had. In the olden days, some slave descendants owned businesses. Black businesspersons were highly respected because they were able to hire their own people. During this special period, welfare wasn't the norm and was definitely frowned on. It meant those who received assistance weren't capable of fending for themselves and their family. In short, they didn't measure up.

When slave descendants were making a small amount of headway, they were too proud to beg for welfare and were ashamed for *anyone* to know their family had to receive handouts to exist. Then all of a sudden the few small business "Negroes" had built up in their communities was taken away with the stroke of a pen. The administration called it Urban Renewal.

Nowadays, slave deccendants don't own their fair share of businesses; therefore, they can't hire their own people and, unfortunately, white and immigrant businesses have unfair employment practices. Negative circumstances, over which unaware slaves had no control, caused welfare to become routine in the black community forcing what little pride slaves had to fall by the wayside.

There is no pride in belonging to the poorest, most downtrodden group of unemployed people in a commercial setting that boasts freedom. Unemployment is causing self pride to dissipate at the same pace that welfare is becoming commonplace. America is actually allowing *and even encouraging* welfare to gradually replace employment in the black community. This means welfare is issued to *individual* slaves in order for the *slave culture* to exist and "African American" leaders haven't said a word. Could it be they don't realize this obvious, regressive failure? Don't they know that it's more cost-effective to teach people how to be productive than it is to pay them welfare to stay ignorant, nonproductive and eventually become self destructive?

> *Nowadays, slave descendants don't own their fair share of businesses; therefore, they can't hire their own people and, unfortunately, white and immigrant businesses have unfair employment practices. Negative circumstances, over which unaware slaves had no control, caused welfare to become routine in the black community forcing what little pride slaves had to fall by the wayside.*

In other American cultures, the male species stands proudly at the heads of households *as men* simply because they are in a position to take care of their families. Providing for ones family is an important part of the American dream. The real American dream, however, is a lot larger than one individual family. It's about cultures being able to employ their people and fend for their own kind in a nation that promises peace and prosperity and understands how to achieve it! American Slaves as a culture has never been in a position to employ their people. Slaves weren't allowed to own wealth and, since slavery still hasn't been rectified, slave descendants still don't have access to their fair share of America's prosperity. Without access to their birthright, American Slaves couldn't pass wealth on to their offspring.

It was forbidden for slaves to own *anything* of value. They couldn't even own their individual bodies. When the chains were finally removed from slaves' physical being and they gained possession of their bodies, their culture still couldn't cash in on their people's most apparent attributes: the specialized training they received during slavery: the physical strength that was bred into slaves: and the superb bodies slave masters carefully crafted. The most qualified slaves are still being bought and sold as merchandise to other cultures on the open market. It's called gainful employment, which is an individual endeavor but, in due course, it impacts cultures.

Mentally prepared slaves are hired to run companies for whites or either selected to perform other specialized tasks that enrich whites. The physically strongest and most agile slaves are bought and sold to perform on football fields, in gymnasiums and other gladiator arenas; then there is the music and dance industry. There are many areas of commerce that American Slaves could rightfully control because of why and how they were bred and what went into their breeding. Unfortunately, because of inherited ignorance and malignant division, slaves don't realize that working together they could control many related industries. They could actually control their own destiny!

When slave descendants acquire wealth, some of them try to give back to their culture. Unfortunately, slaves have never understood

America's monetary system enough to know how it really works; therefore, they have no idea how to "give back." For instance, it's common to see athletes and other wealthy slave descendants on TV advertising that they are "giving back" to their people. This is a *huge* misconception. These chosen few don't even know who their people are. They are not giving back, especially to their people! They are slaves who think they are "African Americans." They are not giving; they are getting! They're being paid to advertise for white companies! Giving money to charities and splinter groups and advertising for white conglomerates doesn't benefit their people at all. The advertisement might even feature slave children as recipients but this is misleading and deceptive also.

It's vitally important that whites *and* blacks understand how to effectively "give back" if their desire is to help the slave culture. Slave descendants are so screwed up, the upper crusts don't know how to help or either they don't want to help, and the lower-class don't understand what true help really is. If truth be told, it's doubtful they will understand that what they are reading at *this very moment* is the main help they need. ASI is giving back to slave descendants in the purest form. We are supplying the *desperately* needed intelligence that unaware slaves have *always* needed!

Mr. Charlie, you're up!

The prevailing power structure is the only entity that has the authority to put a stop to ignorant leaders succeeding each other and ignorant leadership succeeding itself. The proper rectification of slavery dictates that the governing body allows the slave culture to be included in America's budget and permitted to function under the patronage and guidance of an ironclad development plan that will elevate the Slave Nation but will still benefit America. The problem here is "African American" leaders don't understand what any of this means and members of the power structure of America, those with the wherewithal to sanction the American Slave Movement, are descended from those who committed the crime of slavery. If they had any decency and wanted to rectify slavery, they would have done it long ago. They're bound to know slavery needs rectifying. This tells us that because slave descendants were subjugated and still reside in the same oppressive setting where they were enslaved, the documentation that defines their freedom must be prepared by a third party or either drawn up by the astute leaders of the oppressed people. It could then be refined by those who oppose rectifying slavery but who still have the ability to understand simplicity. The simple fact is: For America to remain a stable country, slavery must be rectified.

Having no concept of business and not understanding their true ethnicity, "African American" leaders repudiate a legitimate advancement program for slaves but welcome programs that are welfare-grounded and subsidized by our government for "African Americans." It's only natural that a leader who doesn't understand business would think welfare is free money, but it's not. In an industrial society, a red flag automatically goes up at the mention free money because it cost the recipient too much!

ASI's mission is to teach slave descendants how to overcome the free mind-set because it destroys aggression and stops the competing process. Slaves have always loved to compete. It didn't matter that the master was right behind them threatening them with his whip; picking more cotton and 'toting that bale' the farthest and fastest was still a point of pride for slaves — if for no other reason than it gave the fastest slaves bragging rights that they outran a flogging. Slave descendants just never had the chance to get into fair economic competition that rewards them fairly and their entire culture justly.

Now that we have a clearer understanding of slave descendants plight, ASI gladly accepts the challenge of forging the way. The time has finally arrived for the slave culture to move forward. It all boils down to two words: *American Slaves!* They were bred in America and survived a very complicated beginning but they're still here and, considering the circumstances, alive and well! The Civil War was simply God's way of announcing the beginning of the American Slave Nation!

We are now ready to proceed. ❖

CHAPTER

2

The "American Slave Movement"

(The price of freedom is staggering and clearly misunderstood, but it shouldn't be feared)

Gatekeeper in the mayor's office

Charting a course that will guide slave descendants out of mental bondage and into mainstream America is an ambitious undertaking that must be done in phases. The intention is for slave descendants to become a profitable, self-sustaining culture. ASI will start out by structuring an advancement vehicle in the form of an organization to guide slave descendants through the beginning stages of the American Slave Movement. This will include their awakening, proper identification and the initiation of the litigation of slavery.

To structure a profit-making organization in America, several important items go into its formulation. Among these are to be legalized and properly registered with the correct authority. For a controversial project of this nature and magnitude to succeed, it is absolutely necessary that American leaders in positions of authority, white and black, be notified of what is taking place and be kept up to speed on each move slave descendants make so they can know why tactical steps are being taken: blacks so they won't start acting like crabs in a barrel and block ASI's advancement: and whites so they can sanction the American Slave Movement and guide our effort.

Slave descendants can't merge into mainstream America unless black leaders stop blocking the doorway. Forward progress won't be smooth and effective unless whites in key positions endorse the American Slave Movement, monitor ASI's development and document slave descendants' growth.

The reason why the American Slave Movement must involve whites at the forefront of rectifying slavery is because slave breeding in America was a *white undertaking*. The reason why rectifying slavery has become a black responsibility is slavery was never rectified and blacks are the ones who are suffering the most because of 'non-rectification.' Whites have shown they are ready for slave descendants to grow up and assume their rightful position in America, but a word of caution: When American Slaves start moving forward, they must exercise due vigilance because Uncle Toms will run straight to whites and automatically badmouth those they will identify as "ringleaders."

If the rectification of slavery looks like a slave uprising is being initiated or if a black takeover appears to be underway, the movement won't work. Paralleling present day to when slavery was in full bloom, misinformation would make it would look like slaves got together, planned an escape and were plotting to break free! Of course that was during slavery, when slaves were considered valuable property. American Slaves breaking free now, with reparations staring them in the face, would be parallel to an unwanted child of the wealthiest family in the world preparing to run away from home. "African American" family members who understand what American Slaves' bequest really is will gladly help you pack and be thankful when *all* American Slaves are gone: It leaves more for them, real immigrants and minorities.

Recognizing American Slaves' Ace in the hole

White Americans are the controlling culture in America. They are also the parent culture of American Slaves. America is the parent country and motherland of the American Slave culture. American Slaves, Inc. is the legal representative of the American Slave Nation. This tells us, among other things, that white Americans must sanction American Slaves' freedom and be at the forefront of the movement. What it all boils down to is *slaves can't be free unless white America says so!* Without thinking it all the way through,

"African American" leaders probably won't agree with that assessment; even though the whole world knows the statement to be true. If white Americans, the dominant culture, don't want Descendants of American Slaves to be mentally, morally and financially free, American Slaves' mental condition will perpetuate; their depressed outlook will remain unchanging; their financial situation will worsen right out in the open, and there won't be a thing "African Americans" can do about it. Marching and carrying signs won't get the job done. "Negroes" already tried that. Changing slave descendants collective name again won't work either; that's what's currently contributing to their failure.

During slavery, slaves couldn't break free without the help of whites or assistance from institutions run by whites. Today, slave descendants can't enter mainstream America without the help and approval of whites.

Incorporating the slave culture into corporate America so they can operate legally and structuring American Slaves to become financially solvent in a business setting has never been done before but it's still a doable task. The average American might not realize it but we already know how to free slaves. We gained this experience from engaging in wars to free cultures in other parts of the world. ASI is going about freeing American Slaves a little differently, though. Instead of war, our epitome is peace, a relatively new concept considering the negative connotation. Freeing American Slaves in a peaceful manner in a society that is untrustworthy and has been proven to be unfair is a process that we must feel our way through as if we are in the middle of a "minefield."

Realizing the devastation that could be caused by a young child being abandoned in a heartless adult setting and now understanding that the slave culture is a young nation and their unaware leaders are their main hindrance, we simply parallel what should be done to eradicate a young child's plight and then apply that same method to a group of abandoned slaves.

We now have a definite starting point

We will kick off the American Slave Movement and chart slave descendants' course as if the Civil War is just now ending and slaves are being released. The scene unfolds as American Slaves are being told who they are and what is in store for them as America's only offspring. We must exercise patience and keep in mind that the slaves are still ignorant. They won't understand any of what is going on but that's to be expected. It's the same as when a child first starts in school and is greeted by caring teachers who understand the situation. Their job is to prepare the children to function in a cruel society.

Descendants of American Slaves have been identified and are getting their first instructions on how to be a functional entity in America, a country that was founded on business and built on the backs of American Slaves who just happen to be their forebears.

This book is being written not only to inform slave descendants of what has taken place thus far in the movement but also to prepare them so they can enjoy a bright future. The overall message is that Descendants of American Slaves inherited an obligation: They owe it to their forebears to take control of their destiny. So, stand up! *Step up to the plate* — and swing the bat smartly! Do not *under any circumstances* allow weak, *useless* leaders to hold you back!

Man your post! Here they come!

Hope is a powerful motivator. Without hope, there is no honest exertion. Unfortunately, slaves have never had hope, so a healthy dose of what they can look forward to will spur them forward. The first injection of hope into the American Slave Movement is that ASI is a new, small company with zero net worth. We make that statement not in shame and pity but with American pride. We want all Americans to know where we started and, in the end, know that ASI believed in the American dream and set out to prove that it is alive and well. American Slaves started with nothing — but working together they can excel!

We will start chasing the American dream by alerting the American public that American Slaves have a God-given right to participate in the human race and to compete for America's wealth and chase the

American dream *even more so than immigrant cultures!*

ASI is giving due notice that American Slaves, Inc., the official vehicle that was specifically designed to merge slave descendants into mainstream America, was incorporated in Frankfort, Kentucky, the Capitol, and is in good standing with the governing body. The American Slave Movement, however, was started in Louisville, where the founder resides. This legal incorporating merged American Slaves with commercial America. Slave descendants now have the key to mainstream American. They still aren't allowed to participate in the mainstream as a unit because they don't understand how to work in unison, mainly because they haven't been tutored and they have no racial pride.

We have already instilled a small amount of hope into the movement, just enough optimism to get us in gear, but it's going to take pride to get people who have been depressed to rise up and start running. It's crucial that slave descendants understand their racial importance. Pride in who they are will encourage slaves to speak with one voice; not an easy task to achieve considering it took hundreds of years for American Slaves to be born and come this far. The pace should quicken now because then slaves had no plan; now ASI has an advancement diagram. We have astute leaders calling the shots who have been trained to think at a higher level. Slavery might not be straightened out in any of our lifetimes. It is the duty, nonetheless, of current generations to make sure America takes the necessary steps so it will be straightened out in its predestined time.

If America wants her slaves to be completely free, the shame of slavery must be reversed and the stain it left in the fabric of America must be erased. For this to happen, American institutions must work together for the common cause. It's the job of American slaves, Inc. to show America at large how this can be accomplished.

Moving forward

After being incorporated in Frankfort, Kentucky, and being granted a Sinking Fund license in Louisville, ASI acquired 501 (c) (3) certification with the Internal Revenue Service in Cincinnati, Ohio. The next step became to gain political endorsement from the nearest governing body.

To get the approval of city fathers, ASI arranged an appointment with the mayor of Louisville. Unfortunately, instead of being able to meet with the mayor, the delegation was steered to Louisville's head gatekeeper in the mayor's office. Thus began ASI's unrelenting, seemingly unending bout with lethargic gatekeepers. We found them to be shamefully interesting.

ASI being stood up by the mayor and then steered to a subordinate figurehead caused the meeting to get off to a rocky start. After telling the mayor's aide the purpose of our visit and supplying him with our hastily put together brochure that explained slave descendants' proper identity and ASI's mission, for reason that later became evident, things went downhill from there. The Deputy Mayor became offended; remarking that "white politicians don't care about a bunch of black folks who don't vote," adding that he couldn't get involved with a herd of black people running around town calling themselves slaves; that he had his family to think about. He became highly insulted when a member of our delegation suggested that he was a slave descendant.

It's unfortunate that when some slave descendants reach the level of gatekeeper, they become ashamed of their culture and afraid to speak up for their own people. Once they rise up and become the cream of the crop of the "African American" culture, they hide behind the immigrant charade and lower themselves to the depth of scoundrel playing it safe as Uncle Toms. Hoping to secure their immediate families only, their effort now goes into protecting their positions in the workplace. Lack of commonsense coupled with introversion causes them to reject helping the people they left behind in ignorance in an industrial setting. They stand guard at the many doors of opportunity in industry but they won't allow the slave culture access. They will, however, let certain slaves in but only if they claim they are "African Americans." Ignorant slaves who don't understand their proper identity have no allegiance to their true ethnicity.

There are too many slave descendant families that need guidance for

"African Americans" who are supposed to be leaders of *people* to be limited to gloating about their accomplishments as an individual provider. Their culture, which is the foundation that allowed them to be a provider, is going to "hell in a hand-basket!"

Many strong black men who have the potential to be great leaders of *people* surrender to weakness and spend their entire lives in fear. They wind up wasting their capabilities and potential on a single person just because they are immediate family! It's disgraceful for slave descendants who calls themselves leaders of *people* to be so small-minded they don't have the ability or bigness to help anyone but their immediate families. Without even realizing it, they have become useless Uncle Toms who have been tricked with double-talk, hoodwinked by success, led astray because of ignorance, and then cut out of the herd by the masters. They hate *anyone* who tells them the simple truth that they are backward leaders!

Gatekeepers in the political arena at large

Politicians are usually described in one of two ways. Number 1: a person experienced in the art or science of government; especially one actively engaged in conducting the business of a government. Number 2: a person engaged in party politics as a profession primarily interested in political office for selfish or other narrow, usually short-sighted reasons.

"African American" politician in Louisville, Kentucky, fall into category 2. They point fingers at their counterparts because problems don't get solved and then bully their constituency for having problems. When they are confronted with real problems that affect slave descendants, they usually try to stay out of sight, keep their heads down, and through it all — they still refuse to think!

"African American" politicians prove they don't understand how to lead an ethnic group of people by not understanding how to follow a single leader from within their group. Oh, sure, they know how to tag along behind their white bosses and carry out their orders verbatim. That's not thinking, leading or following in regard to their group. Cultural thinking is when you tackle tough problems that hamper your group and figure out how to solve them. Leading is when you rally the people around problems and motivate them into corrective action. Following is when you put forth effort to see that orders given by another leader who is trying to rectify slavery are carried out. Not one "African American" politician has even tried to follow up on Benjamin Franklin's cry for justice for the slave culture. This is evidenced by not one of them introducing a bill that will accomplish that end.

If "African American" leaders were to introduce a bill in honor of *American Slaves* or their descendants, we would at least know they are trying to think. Benjamin Franklin was the first top-ranking official to attempt negotiating on behalf of American Slaves, and he was a white man.

In 1787, when he served as president of the Pennsylvania Society for Promoting the Abolition of Slavery, he sent Congress a petition on behalf of the Society asking for the abolition of slavery and an end to the slave trade. The petition, signed on February 3, 1790, asked the first Congress, then meeting in New York City, to "devise means for removing the inconsistency from the character of the American People," and to "promote mercy and justice toward this distressed race." The petition was introduced to the House on February 12 and to the Senate on February 15, 1790. It was immediately denounced by pro-slavery congressmen and sparked a heated debate in both the House and the Senate. The Senate took no action on the petition, and the House referred it to a select committee for further consideration. On March 5, 1790, the committee claimed that the Constitution restrained Congress from prohibiting the importation or emancipation of slaves until 1808 and then the committee tabled the petition. On April 17, 1790, just two months later, at the age of 84, before he could fulfill his inherited obligation to American Slaves, Benjamin Franklin died, and not one "African American" politician followed up on what Benjamin Franklin was trying to accomplish!

"African American" politicians are in *perfect* positions to advance the slave culture into mainstream America. In fact, it's their jobs to introduce legislation that would move slave descendants forward. Why else did they run for political office to do what whites tell them to do? Then why did they run for reelection, to do what has always been done — or just to help their immediate families? There is an old adage that "ignorance of the law is no excuse." Even though ASI functions within that principle, as the representative company of the slave culture, we totally disagree with the saying. Nevertheless, thus far, ASI has put up with this nonsense and allowed weak leaders to escape our wrath using *ignorance* as an excuse long enough — but no more. Since ASI has offered *America's Little Black Book,* the missing intelligence that inept politicians needed, at their disposal, they can no longer claim ignorance as an excuse for not helping their people.

Gatekeepers at the Chamber of Commerce

After running into a stumbling block at the mayor's office, which is the executive branch of government in Louisville, ASI's next stop was Greater Louisville, Inc. *(the Louisville Area Chamber of Commerce).* On August 20, 2009, ASI secured a meeting with the president of Greater Louisville, Inc. At that meeting, ASI was afforded the opportunity of paralleling slave descendants' deteriorating condition to the budding condition of other nationalities by paralleling the leadership of other nationalities to that of slave descendants. It became abundantly clear that the gatekeeper hypothesis sprang *directly* from the Uncle Tom foundation. It was chilling to find out the real reason why slave descendants aren't represented in American money matters.

Since the meeting at the mayor's office, ASI had been analyzing why slave descendants continue to lag so far behind other nationalities in commerce. We had been giving some serious thought to how things went down and were wondering exactly where the mayor stood when it comes to the welfare of slave descendants. Prior to meeting with the mayor, ASI made sure the city leader, his wife, the chief of police and other dignitaries had autographed copies of *America's Little Black Book.* We wanted the mayor and other public figures to understand *beforehand* that ASI understood some of Louisville's black problems and we had a plan that would solve the most prevailing one: young "African Americans" seemingly turning wild!

We were now wondering if any of Louisville's leaders actually read the book. Maybe the mayor didn't deal with black problems at all. He could just show up for a few minutes at black functions as part of his routine to court slave descendants' votes. ASI was also curious whether gatekeepers were called in to control the outcome of all meetings that involve slave descendants, aka "African Americans." These thoughts having been discussed at ASI prior to the meeting at the chamber, it didn't surprise our small delegation when an "African American," accompanying the chamber president, was introduced as a vice president of the business group.

The president of the chamber appeared glad to see us; he was all smiles. The vice president, hearing we were there representing Descendants of American Slaves, was surprised and clearly embarrassed. The second he heard the word 'slave,' his eyebrows arched and a scowl came over his face. During the course of the meeting, showing great humiliation, he grudgingly admitted that he *probably* was descended from slaves. Having to literally pull this simple truth out of him in front of his white boss illustrated he was ashamed of who he was. He obviously didn't understand the consequences of his ethnic birthright even though ASI had given his boss *America's Little Black Book* during the same time frame that we gave the mayor and the chief of police their copies. ASI reasoned if his boss had read it, surely he would have shared the information with his staff — especially a *vice president* who mistakenly thinks he's an "African American."

Slave descendant who hold influential positions but don't realize their true ethnicity and understand the power of their rank, knowingly or unknowingly, are a gatekeepers; simply because they are in the right position to represent their own people, Descendants of American Slaves, but they instead impersonate foreigners by portraying themselves as "African Americans." That's contemptible ignorance!

Dr. King told "Negroes" to go into business: Business is commerce: Chambers of commerce represents businesses! As vice president of Louisville's chamber of commerce, the *business* group no less, it is his *direct* inherited duty to help guide slave descendants, *no matter what they are called,* into mainstream America simply because America is a commercial country — and he's the HNIC (head nigger in charge) of guarding the gate.

His title, vice president of the business group, makes him a head gate-keeper at the entrance of Louisville's economic arena. His attitude puts him smack-dab in the line of fire and he doesn't even know it. A person in his position who is unaware of his own culture and ashamed of his earthly existence doesn't have the motivation and certainly not the mettle to be a racial leader in a biased commercial setting like Louisville, Kentucky, where discrimination is the norm. He doesn't seem to realize that it's his people who are being abused and discriminated against in the commercial environment that *he* presides over. His unknowing puts slave descendants at a distinct disadvantage in America's business arena, the economic battlefield that Dr. King spoke of.

On the other hand, since he didn't consider himself to be a slave descendant, maybe he didn't consider himself to be a racial leader who is representing slave descendants, either. If that is the case, he should be removed from his position because, whether he knows it or not, he is the chamber's "token black." To further attest to this vice president's confusion and backwardness, he compared American Slaves, Inc., the organization that represents his own people, Descendants of American Slaves, to the Ku Klux Klan!

ASI finds it highly offensive that a person in his position would make such an irrational remark. You would think the vice president of Louisville's *Chamber of Commerce* would be an educated person and be somewhat rational, or at least have the ability to learn simple things. What has the chamber been teaching this guy? ASI finds it surprising that an educated person *who is descended from slaves* doesn't know the difference between American Slaves and the Ku Klux Klan! Is the Chamber of Commerce a haven where discriminatory ignorance is taught? With no other information to contradict this assumption, ASI takes for granted they are. Why else would they have a slave descendant who thinks he is an "African American" guarding the gate to opportunity and shooing *knowledgeable* Descendants of American Slaves away from the door except to make sure ignorance and discrimination stays firmly in place?

Another manager at the chamber, who is not a slave descendant, heard the vice president had openly made this awful remark in the presence of his staff, instructing them to relay the message to ASI. He promised ASI a written apology for the unfavorable comment. As of this writing, ASI has not received this apology. Did the chamber intervene to make sure ASI didn't have such damning, written evidence in our possession? Keep in mind, America is a legal society that is controlled by detailed paperwork and proper documentation. A written apology is legal documentation.

If the American Slave culture is to advance into mainstream America in a peaceful manner, "African Americans" who hold leadership positions in the commercial arena must understand the full impact of their positions in regard to their racial origin. They must value the fact that it was *their* foreparents who were baptized in ignorance and intentionally indoctrinated with a slave mentality. When ignorance is planted in unaware minds, it will germinate and carry forward expeditiously: The chamber's vice president and Louisville's Deputy Mayor are prime examples. Ignorance comes in many forms, is widespread and growing. There is no shame in being ignorant, fellows; the shame is in staying ignorant in the midst of an intelligent society.

The reason why American Slaves, Inc. wanted to meet with the Mayor was to alert him of ASI's intent to merge slave descendants into mainstream America launching them from the city of Louisville. We were meeting with the chamber of commerce to discuss slave descendants *re-entering* commercial America through the chamber's door. Using chambers of commerce as slave descendants' entryway is the best way for ASI to merge the slave culture into the American mainstream so they can be woven into the commercial fabric of America properly.

The fault lies within

According to *America's Little Black Book,* pages 78, 105, 115, and 161, any black person in a position of authority that affects the advancement of Descendants of American Slaves must be held accountable not only to their places of employment but also to their people. Leadership accountability must start immediately. As a result, ASI will make derisory leaders aware of the American Slave Movement. The response we receive from them will determine our next move. If it is positive, we will include them in the movement and move forward without delay. If leaders react in an adverse, unhelpful way, we will take time out and make those who don't have the potential to be *proper* leaders uncomfortable in their leadership positions.

American Slaves, Inc. is not the Ku Klux Klan nor a militant group or a fly-by-night company. *America's Little Black Book* and other books that helped launch the American Slave Movement were not published to incite rage or anger other nationalities. They were written to expose gatekeeper barriers and give details about the ignorance that keeps the slave culture hamstrung in a commercial setting. The books explain in simple terms what *must* be done to alleviate America's racial situation in a peaceful manner.

This book is not written to be a personal attack on the chamber of commerce or any other company. ASI is not attempting to smear any "African American's" good name. Our effort is to get vital information into the hands of every leader, white and black, who cares about the well-being of America — especially the situation Descendants of American Slaves have wound up in. American Slaves started out at the bottom of the barrel and have been unjustly kept there ever since! It's about time we Americans did something about it.

"African Americans" in leadership positions who aren't functioning at capacity or who don't have slave descendants' best interests at heart, adversely affect the advancement of the slave culture. They, therefore, become prime targets for exposure and fair game to authentic leaders. ASI doesn't have the authority to force inadequate leaders to live up to their inherited responsibility to their people; ASI does have an obligation to point out obstacles that hinder slave descendants' progress with *extreme* prejudice. High-up positions held by "African Americans" at the many chambers of commerce in America (and all other organizations that are key to the American Slave Movement) are far too important to the advancement of slave descendants to remain covered up and kept ineffective. Slave descendants' racial decline dictates that ASI alter its advancement tactics by vigorously opposing and then exposing those who hinder Descendants of American Slaves' progress.

Chambers of commerce represents corporate America. Businesses that belong to these chambers have the might and the right to contribute to worthwhile causes, which ASI truly is. Justifiable contributions could help pave the way to true emancipation for a group of depressed American people who have been dejected far too long. Who is more qualified to benefit from corporate America's overflow of bounty than Descendants of American Slaves? Slaves were bred on American soil and physically enslaved and mentally abused for the *sole* purpose of helping to build corporate America. Why not use the overflow of bounty from corporate America to help rectify slavery? This straightforward, *uncomplicated* solution to merging slave descendants into mainstream America has been right before our eyes since the conclusion of corporal slavery but, because of greed, ignorance and apathy, is overlooked by American leaders, including slave descendants' own nearsighted, gluttonous leaders. It's a leader's responsibility to bring the needs of his group to America's attention. Faulty "African American" leadership is clearly the reason why America Slaves are denied access to mainstream America!

Gatekeepers at United Way

Even though American Slaves were bred in American and are 100% American-made, slave descendants still wound up being second-class citizens in their homeland. Second-class citizens aren't in a position to access America's wealth. Yet, on a daily basis, slave descendants encounter opportunities that could lead to their achieving the American dream and could expedite their becoming first-class citizens. Unfortunately, because slaves were never taught how America really operates, grassroots slaves don't recognize chance encounters as gates of opportunity. ASI found out however that some of these *same* chance opportunities that benefit individuals could very well benefit the slave culture making it possible for all slaves to reach true freedom and easier for individual slaves to achieve the American dream.

In America, the aftereffects of slavery are clearly evident and racial bias is abundant. Underhanded acts of discrimination, however, are usually carefully disguised. Because of tradition, slave descendants, thinking they have no recourse when they run into camouflaged blockades, usually take sly unfairness and snide rejection in stride. Easily placated because assimilation is firmly in place, the average slave feels that's the way it is and the way it's always been. Slave descendants are continually steered away from avenues that lead to accomplishment and are directed to barriers set up by gatekeepers.

ASI will give an illustration how the cultural screening process *really* works and show the reader one of the many sly but clever ways "African American" leaders routinely block slave descendants from gaining access to mainstream America: The early part of August 2009, ASI was denied the opportunity to share in an event that United Way sponsored. If ours had been an individual effort, instead of American Slaves, Inc. fending for the slave culture, we probably would have just taken our individual rejection in stride and kept moving on. But this was not a selfish undertaking and, because ASI suspected this same type of unfairness is the norm all across America; we felt duty bound to understand the fullness of the rejection. Depending on the information we uncovered, the fate of the American Slave Nation could very well hang in the balance. That's how weak the slave culture really is. So, instead of taking this particular denial in stride, we stopped long enough to ask why — *why is ASI being rejected?* Why won't Metro United Way let American Slaves through the door? Metro United Way is funded by slave descendants' dollars, also! Why aren't slave descendants allowed to share in the wealth they helped create and participate in the country they helped build?

Metro United Way had created the LIVE UNITED Social Innovation

Prize. There was a grand prize of $10,000 to be awarded for a solution that produces results solving social problems. It sounded quite interesting because, if there ever was a social problem that needs solving, it's the aftereffects of slavery. So ASI entered the contest. Judges were to select finalists in July. In early August, finalists would be contacted and there would be interviews, coaching and polishing. The introduction to the prize read:

"Everyone deserves opportunities to have a good life: a quality education that leads to a stable job, enough income to support a family through retirement, and good health. That's why Metro United Way's work is focused on the building blocks for a good life. To be successful, our community needs to think differently about our approaches. We need to harness the wide-ranging talents of our best social pioneers — encouraging them to innovate and pursue their visions. As in the business sector, there is no shortage of innovators, but there is not yet enough systematic support available to social innovators. Metro United Way encourages and supports the work of pragmatic visionaries who achieve sustainable social change through a new invention, a different approach, a more rigorous application of known technologies or strategies, or a combination of these. The LIVE UNITED Social Innovation Prize is for expenses directly related to the implementation of the solution, and will help attract funding and other resources and support. Finalists will be offered nurturing and support to incubate their solutions. Each finalist will be connected to a "wisdom council" of mentors and advisors with whom the finalist may meet regularly. The wisdom council will be empowered to connect the finalists with additional resources for advice, training, and support. For many of the social entrepreneurs who participate in the competition, the wisdom council and additional connection to resources will be more valuable than the prize."

As you can see, the LIVE UNITED Social Innovation Prize was tailor-made for American Slaves, Inc. Judging was to be done in two phases. Initial screening and selection of finalists was to be done by a panel of volunteers who had indicated their willingness to serve on wisdom councils. Finalists were to be posted on Metro United Way's website and assigned to education, income, health or combination categories. Visitors to the website could even donate by credit card to one or more finalist. To encourage broad participation, minimum donations would be kept as small as is feasible. Winners would be determined by the highest total donations in each category. All finalists would receive the amount donated to their solutions.

$10,000 might not sound like much considering what America owes the slave culture or what ASI is attempting to accomplish but, after struggling for so many years keeping the American Slave Movement alive and now running out of funds, this sounded too good to be true! ASI had never even considered that large concerns such as United Way were doing the same thing as ASI — with a couple of huge differences: United Way has wealth, power and influence; they can make things happen. ASI is a new corporation and as of yet has neither wealth nor power. Another difference is United Way doesn't recognized slave descendants as an American culture; ASI's every effort is spent in honor of the American Slave culture — and this prize was right down our alley — and just in the nick of time!

In the end, ASI didn't win. We didn't even come in second. Then ASI found out we weren't even considered! How could that be? ASI is going straight to the core of America's racial predicament to solve the mother of all social problems, human bondage and mind manipulation that was carried out right here in America! The evidence is everywhere! Completely baffled, ASI representatives requested and, to our surprise, received feedback why we weren't considered. Following is a condensed version of how and why ASI arrived at the conclusion that it was gate-keepers who stood in the way of American Slaves, Inc. even being considered for receiving assistance from United Way.

Cutting to the chase

August 20, 2009, ASI sent Mr. Howard Mason, Director of Community Building at Metro United Way, a letter explaining that, after reading the feedback from the judges of LIVE UNITED explaining why we weren't considered, for clarification purposes, ASI thought it was necessary that we respond to their comments why they didn't consider our innovation:

> **Judge number 1 wrote:** *"I believe this project perpetuates racism, enabling, and asks us to suspend our intelligence — despite our race — and justify allowing a certain segment of the population to blame historical occurrences as the reason for a lack of current success."*

ASI's response: American Slaves, Inc. does *not* perpetuate racism; nor do we ask anyone to suspend their intelligence. The purpose of American Slaves, inc. is to enhance the overall intelligence of America at large by seeking the truth and then sharing this wisdom with everyone regardless of race, creed or culture. If we are to rectify the wrong of slavery without it angering the population or destabilizing the American economy, we must be strong enough to accept facts. It is very difficult to explain 400 years of ignorance in just a few sentences. It's doubtful that any of those who judged ASI's innovation had read *America's Little Black Book*. Without this vital information, they wouldn't understand ASI's noble intentions. Mr. Mason, there is a huge difference between placing blame and stating facts. Historical occurrences have always had a profound effect on the present — especially in regard to Descendants of American Slaves, simply because life carries forward. The aftereffects of slavery are clearly evident. I'm simply stating facts, not placing blame. If I were to blame anyone for slave descendants' current lack of success — it would be our own leaders — they still think they are "African Americans!"

Judge 2 wrote: *"I believe this proposal will alienate many local audiences and will ultimately limit its ability to sustain itself."*

ASI's response: ASI's effort to rectify slavery hasn't alienated any local audiences except those slave descendants, aka "African Americans," who have their own personal agendas and are afraid of the consequences of their own actions. Ultimately, the truth must surface, and it will prevail. In 2009, *American Slaves, Inc. Renaissance Plan, The Next Step Forward,* was published. It explains slavery in a different, more positive light. It illustrates how the aftereffects of slavery can be rectified without negative confrontations and consequences. All we ask of other American cultures is to wish us well. The publication *American Slaves, Inc. Renaissance Plan* explains clearly how our plan can sustain itself.

Judge 3 wrote: *"I was initially put off by the organization name and somewhat confused by the writing style and what seemed to me to be a patronizing and secretive tone. Once I re/read through the proposal and visited the organization's website the simplicity and honesty of the idea became clearer. Honest and informative conversation and education about American slavery - it hasn't been done."*

ASI's response: Unfortunately, sometimes, the truth really is stranger than fiction. The aftereffects of human bondage, servile oppression and mental contamination remain unexplored, festering in plain sight seemingly unnoticed. If ASI appears to be strange, it's only because slavery has been covered up, while ASI is open and honest. We won't deviate from the truth just because it appears strange to those who aren't acquainted with facts or who try to avoid reality. We are grateful to the one judge who took the time to visit our web site. It helped him to realize that "talking openly about slavery hadn't been done before," which is innovation within itself. It is not ASI's intention to be patronizing and we are definitely not secretive. ASI is a down-to-earth, 501 (c) (3) organization. Every board meeting is videotaped; accurate minutes are kept and are available to those who are interested in knowing what phase the movement is in. We want all Americans to know and understand what we are doing and how we are doing it — and become involved. All we ask is a little help and understanding from those who are in the position to help and who are paid to lead the way — starting with educators.

On with the show

The reason why ASI responded to United Way in such a manner is we didn't want a powerful organization like this to misunderstand our intentions. Suppose the vice president of Louisville's Chamber of Commerce had spread the word that ASI truly is the Ku Klux Klan. That would be devastating to the American Slave Movement. Better yet, suppose he was one of the judges on the panel? At least that would explain why ASI's innovation was rejected. To follow up and hopefully have ASI's creativeness re-evaluated, a meeting was arranged with Mr. Howard Mason, Director of Community Building at Metro United Way. In attendance were Mr. Mason, Mr. Norris Shelton, president of American Slaves, Inc., Mr. Virgil Boyd, executive director of ASI, and Mr. Marcel Cabrera, a board member of ASI.

Mr. Mason seemed to be a nice man and was very open with us. Most whites are. He said, because ASI's innovation was so original, LIVE UNITED Social Innovation Prize called in "special judges" to judge ASI's proposal. We requested names, but he declined to tell us who the special judges were. During the course of our meeting, though, he told us that he understood our mission and wanted to be of assistance. As the meeting wore on and everyone got comfortable, we discussed gatekeepers, gatekeeper institutions and the damage they do to slave descendants, to the slave culture and therefore to America. We wanted Mr. Mason to know that ASI suspected there was more to our rejection than what the judges wrote and what we were being told. Trying to be helpful and let us know that United Way wasn't a gatekeeper institution and wasn't to blame for ASI's innovation not being considered, Mr. Mason told us if we really wanted assistance, we should contact Dr. J. Blaine Hudson, professor at the University of Louisville and chairman of the Department of Pan African Studies — case closed! It was clear to see that we had been weeded out and setback again and this time, even though we couldn't be absolutely sure, we had a pretty good idea which gatekeeper had weeded us out.

ASI doesn't want to "jump-the-gun" and wrongly accuse anyone but, until that moment, we had no idea that the gatekeeper system had such broad-reaching, overlapping, negative consequences. This particular name keeps popping up everywhere we go — even in *unrelated* areas! Unaware gatekeepers are strangling the life out of the entire slave culture on all fronts and it's a safe bet they don't even know they have their people in a choke-hold!

Actually, when you think about, it doesn't matter who the judges were or who the gatekeepers are; innovation is still innovation. It doesn't even matter that it was a grassroots slave who figured out how to rectify slavery and not a high-powered educator. What does matter is if there are funds available to straighten slavery out — what are we waiting for? Let's get on with it! ASI doesn't care who leads slave descendants out of mental bondage so long as we get started and whoever leads lead properly.

Someone that Uncle Toms are willing to listen to needs to tell them about the American Slave Movement, what phase it is in and what they can do to help. Officers at ASI usually run into problems when we solicit help from "African Americans" who are in leadership positions. ASI is open and truthful and we refuse to alter that trait, and gatekeepers are too thin-skinned to hear the bald-faced truth and they obviously refuse to alter that trait. When ASI is fortunate enough to wrangle a meeting out of one of them, we must exercise extra caution. If we are not careful how we explain what is really going on in the movement and also around them in regard to the position they are in, we might say the wrong thing and our effort winds up being for naught, or worse. We always let people in leadership positions know up-front that our effort is not personal. Still, they usually become overly defensive. They either don't understand what we said or they don't believe what they heard.

During these rare meetings, if sensitive leaders seem in a receptive mood, ASI will take a chance and explain their proper identity and point out different gatekeeper positions. This is always tricky because, if we're not vigilant, we stand a good chance of losing the prospect. Telling "African Americans" leaders the truth about ASI's mission and enlightening them of the consequences of their staying unaware in their leadership positions can have dire consequences. Ignorant leaders will instinctively rebel against true help unless it's has the outward appearance of what is already causing their failure.

Misguided disdain for the idea and inherited repugnance because another slave thought up the plan tells them to do whatever is necessary to protect their positions against those who are only trying to help. Not realizing that slavery was business, unwarranted shame tells gatekeepers to deny their slavery heritage and damn those who have the courage to state openly what their destructive ways are doing to their people. Leaders skirting the truth and watering down facts keeps slave descendants submerged in ignorance. Ignorance is the direct cause of poverty and the main supporter of welfare!

White intellectual fortitude

It's is well-documented on the internet and other places of interest that white people *overall* are more knowledgeable than black people or Descendants of American Slaves or whatever slaves are called at the moment. Even the "Kentucky Performance Report," done by the Kentucky Board of Education, bears this out.

In a civilized society, smart people are classified as mentally alert, bright, knowledgeable and shrewd; frequently asking intelligent questions about matters that concern their well-being. Situations that involve masses of people can only be resolved when problems are illuminated and grievances properly aired. As a rule, smart people openly discuss problems that concern their welfare and would only follow astute leadership, which brings us to ASI's next correlation, "smart leaders."

Smart *run-of-the-mill* leaders fall into the *above* category. Smart *racial* leaders, in addition to the above qualities, are forerunners who understand how to follow. They are aware of their surroundings; they keep their followers up to date on issues that control their society, and they understand their *individual* leadership positions in the chain of command. A smart *racial* leader would only follow another smart leader who has a destination mapped out for his people that will enhance their *collective* fate, which brings us to a smart *head* leader. They are a cut above the *average* leader. He or she must have a written plan how they are going to lead their people.

> *A top leader must understand how to construct a stable mode of travel that will carry his group to its pre-planned destination and, realizing the window of opportunity is small, have an approximate time of arrival for all of his people.*

A top leader must understand how to construct a stable mode of travel that will carry his group to its pre-planned destination and, realizing the window of opportunity is small, have an approximate time of arrival for all of his people. This means: "No slave will be left behind — including other leaders!"

Looking at America's racial, financial and spiritual situation, comparatively, Descendants of American Slaves, aka "African Americans," don't appear to be very smart because they have no apparent leadership in place; they have no plan; they aren't moving forward and they don't even know it. There are reasons for this malfunction, however, and an acceptable revamp that will remedy this racial failure: The reason: Slave descendants are being misled. The revamp: They must come to a complete stop, turn around and follow the steps outlined in the *American Slaves, Inc. Renaissance Plan*. It's the only plan in America and the world that is in place — *is totally theirs* — that bears their name! The *American Slaves, Inc. Renaissance Plan* is clearly workable and it won't alienate whites, which brings us to another sticking point.

It's upsetting to most "African American" leaders that ASI openly applauds white effort and at times has relied on whites for direction. There are many reasons for this but ASI will simplify with one straightforward sentence: White folks are in control of America! Some "African American" leaders will even try to deny that which is obvious, which is another sure sign of ignorance. Can you imagine ASI, a slave organization, trying to negotiate the outcome of slavery with "African American" leaders; people who don't even have the capacity to realize who they are or the intelligence to accept the facts of slavery even though the aftereffects are staring them right in the face?

Now, let's look at slavery unemotionally and from a *purely* American point of view, a viewpoint that will no doubt upset "African Americans," also. Wouldn't it be wonderful if American Slaves could have a white leader to guide the slave culture through this stage of infancy? In fact, that would be the ideal situation; simply because slaves were programmed to follow whites long ago and, whether slave descendants like it or not or will admit it or not, this trait has carried forward.

American Slaves, Inc. couldn't have come this far without valid help and pointed direction from caring whites. The only reason why ASI is having so much trouble convincing slave descendants they are *not* "African Americans" is because well-known black leaders haven't given whites the go-ahead to *publicly* confirm that wannabe "African Americans" are in fact Descendants of American Slaves! Once whites get over their trepidation of "African American" leaders and validate the fact that slaves are not "African Americans," slave descendants will gladly accept their true identity and begin to move forward — mainly because whites sanctioned their movement.

Whites already know who slave descendants are. They go along with the "African American" charade because it's free and easy and doesn't cost them anything and slave leaders are too backward to ask for anything for their people using their accurately identifying, cultural name. The average white person's attitude is: If "African American" leaders don't care about advancing the slave culture into mainstream America, why should we?

Having a white leader would make laying the foundation for the slave culture a lot easier. And why not? Slave descendants and whites are blood kin; they share the same bloodline. During the breeding of American Slaves, which took many generations, any white person who could afford the price of a slave could mix his blood with the slave culture at will, and many did. That's why slave descendants wound up being a "multihued" subculture and how whites elevated themselves to being the dominant white culture. Whites owe it to the slave culture to lead slave descendants out of bondage; as the parent culture, it's really their duty.

If a qualified white person were leading the Slave Nation, slave descendants would be in a lot better condition and farther down the road than they are now. After all, we're talking business here. ASI insists that the best, most qualified, person should lead slave descendants. Need more convincing? Compare leadership capabilities. The white culture's strong points are intelligence, brutality, togetherness and tenacity. Whites always employ "KPE:" Knowledge Planning and Execution: They gather Knowledge; they Plan carefully and, if impediments get in the way of Execution, they stand together and use *unrelenting* force until barriers are removed. That's the apex of leadership —getting the job done, period!

On the other side of that same coin, slave descendants are too tenderhearted and too divided to be cohesive in a joint effort. It's a part of their breeding. Slaves can, however, be effective one-on-one, especially toward each other if the master (statutory law) allows it. As a precaution against slaves rising up in rebellion, during the breeding of American Slaves, shrewd planning, intelligence and group alliance were *intentionally* withheld from their group. This says loud and clear that the white culture, by design, is *more* aggressive and *more* intelligent than the slave culture. It also tells us that, because of the white blood slaves inherited, slaves have potential. Unfortunately, their leaders don't have the aptitude to construct a concrete advancement plan so their peoples' potential will have a chance to blossom. Having no idea how to get out of misery, American Slaves' potential has thus far been for naught except on an individual basis. Because of the premeditated intellectual void whites bred into the slave culture, improved intelligence is desperately needed in slave descendants to offset whites' cunning and their unrelenting brutality!

Intelligence has two sides, mental and physical. Being clever and having brainpower are mental aptitudes. In contrast, though, gathering accurate intelligence from the many missing paper trails of history involves putting forth physical effort to make sure information is gathered conceptualized correctly and is disseminated to constituents in a timely fashion in the form of a public address. Gatekeepers are failing miserably in both departments.

To gather intelligence with reference to slavery involves collective thinking. This is not an easy task for slaves because it calls for collaborative effort. To address slave descendants properly, you must address them collectively, and slave descendants are hopelessly divided. To speak to them as a group you must get their attention. To get their attention, you must call them by their accurately identifying surname. To know their name, you must understand their derivation. To understand their derivation or foundation, you must understand the mental transformation and psychological reincarnation that took place in this group of people during the period of slavery when this group was being bred. Only then can leaders be absolutely sure of whom they are addressing and realize what words should be said that will motivate those who are being addressed to act favorably. ❖

CHAPTER 3

Doing the Impossible

(It's impossible only because ASI isn't finished yet)

Black folks working together: fact or fantasy?

Bringing the many splinter groups together that claim to be representing slave descendants is ASI's biggest challenge. If slave descendants understood how to come together and then work in harmony, there would be no gatekeeper system in place unless it was there to keep other cultures from taking advantage of slave descendants.

Splinter groups have no idea how strenuously they work against each other. These groups started competing against each other to represent their perceived culture before their true culture, Descendants of American Slaves, was even formed. This means their effort is largely in vain because the "African American" culture they're vying to represent doesn't even exist! That's why, thus far, it has been impossible to get anything done for slave descendants except paltry welfare and, even then, those issuing the welfare checks won't issue the check in honor of slave descendants or the slave culture. Slaves are instructed to put a check mark in the box that says "African American" or "other."

ASI would like to know why there is no box that says Descendant of American Slaves. Slaves earned the right to have a box of their own and, according to their contribution, it should be at the top of the register. To gain a better understanding of how the slave mentality still controls slave descendants and perpetuates their not working together, we reference a quote from *American Slaves, Inc. Renaissance Plan*, Page 58:

"*To suppress slave uprisings and keep slaves enslaved and*

*slavery ongoing, slave masters programmed their slaves to
never work together unless under the watchful eye of the overseer and to never follow another slave unless the overseer was
in the lead."*

To give an idea when this trait started and illustrate that it is imbedded and has carried forward for hundreds of years without hindrance,
we reference the speech given by "Willie Lynch," a slave owner who over
300 years ago devised a plan to help keep slaves divided and submerged
in ignorance.

Standing on the bank of the James River in 1712, he read aloud a document he had constructed. It became known as the legendary "Willie
Lynch" letter:

> *"Gentlemen, first, I thank the colony of Virginia, for bring-
> ing me here to help you solve some of your problems with
> slaves. Your invitation reached me at my modest plantation
> in the West Indies where I have experimented with some of
> the newest and still the oldest method for control of slaves.
> Ancient Rome would envy us if my program is implemented.
> As our boat sailed south on the James River, named for our il-
> lustrious King James, whose Bible we Cherish, I saw enough to
> know that our problem is not unique. While Rome used cords
> or wood as crosses for standing human bodies along the old
> highways in great numbers, you are here using the tree and
> the rope on occasion.*

> *"I caught the whiff of a dead slave hanging from a tree a
> couple of miles back. You are losing valuable stock by hang-
> ings, you are having uprisings, slaves are running away, your
> crops are sometimes left in the fields too long for maximum
> profit, you suffer occasional fires, your animals are killed,
> Gentleman, you know what your problems are; I do not need
> to elaborate. I am not here to enumerate your problems; I am
> here to introduce you to a method of solving them. In my bag, I
> have a foolproof method for controlling your slaves. I guaran-*

tee every one of you that if installed it will control the slaves for at least three hundred years. My method is simple, any member of your family or any overseer can use it. I have outlined a number of differences among the slaves, and I take these differences and make them bigger. I use fear, distrust, and envy for control purposes.

"These methods have worked on my modest plantation in the West Indies, and it will work throughout the South. Take this simple little list of differences and think about them. On the top of my list is "age" but it is only there because it starts with an "A"; The second is "color" or shade; there is intelligence, size, sex, size of plantation, attitude of owner, whether the slaves live in the valley, on a hill, east or west, north, south, have fine or coarse hair, or is tall or short. Now that you have a list of differences, I shall give you an outline of action, but before that, I shall assure you that distrust is stronger than trust, and envy is stronger than adulation, respect or admiration. The black slave, after receiving this indoctrination, shall carry on and will become self-refueling and self-generating for hundreds of years, maybe thousands. Don't forget, you must pitch the old black versus the young black males, and the young black male against the old black male. You must use the dark skinned slaves versus the light skin slaves. You must use the female versus the male, and the male versus, the female. You must always have your servants and overseers distrust all blacks, but it is necessary that your slaves trust and depend on us. Gentlemen, these kits are your keys to control, use them. Never miss an opportunity. My plan is guaranteed, and the good thing about this plan is that if used intensely for one year the slave will remain perpetually distrustful." William Lynch-1772

After that, we need to back up and regroup

The preceding article is available to the public. It doesn't matter whether the document is authentic or not; it still gives us a *modus ope-randi* how slave masters divided and confused their slaves by planting hate in them. The heritage of imbedded hate is causing slave descendants to evolve alienated and on bad terms with each other. The letter also explains the major weaknesses in the Descendants of American Slaves, aka "African-American," culture today and narrates their perceived destiny: Slave descendants have lost their way and are clearly confused. If they keep on the road they are traveling, they are doomed to failure.

Slaves have gone astray because they have no expectations. Their foreparents were never given any other purpose to be on earth except to be slaves, and the only direction slaves received was to work hard for whites and even harder against each other. Slave descendants still haven't received any direction from America on what is best for the slave culture or which way they should go in order to excel. Indoctrinated with a slave mentality, the program Willie Lynch sold to slave owners was never upgraded from the time when slave masters were at the top of their game and "Uncle Toms" were in place and well-trained.

In 1712, slaves were infused with a defective mind-set fueled by distrust and envy. Distrust is stronger than trust and envy is stronger than adulation, respect or admiration. Armed with this knowledge of how American Slaves' subconscious was controlled then and how slave descendants act toward each other today, we know the plan Willie Lynch was selling was implemented and, according to the laws of adaptation, it carried forward and is still working today, causing ethnic devastation, perpetually. Therefore, *leadership* that can instill hope into the downtrodden is slave descendants' greatest need. Their major hindrance is slaves were taught to never work together and to never follow another slave. Consequently, lack of trust in their own people is their first stumbling block and should be the first thing dealt with; starting with getting their leaders to trust each other enough to work together for a common cause.

Slave masters weren't necessarily concerned with destroying individual slaves who paraded as leaders as you might suspect, and whites of today aren't either. "African American" leaders are harmless. Any slave suspected of being a true leader could be successfully dealt with using extreme violence and not much has changed except a rope then and a bullet now. Confused "African American" leaders that are currently in leadership positions hogging the spotlight are risk-free because, if ignorant leadership is not exposed and properly educated, it will ultimately and *voluntarily* destroy itself anyway or just keep right on procrastinating indefinitely.

Follow the plan — not the man!

The power of leadership is rooted in trust. When trust is damaged or removed and envy is injected, adulation, respect and admiration dissipate. Realizing that slave masters programmed their slaves to never follow another slave, it's important for slave descendants to understand that *following* at this juncture is even more important than leading, simply, because slaves' following another slave is *not* a part of their internal makeup. Slave descendants who become leaders must practice following an authentic leader who has an accepted plan until it becomes an automatic part of their functioning. It will require intelligent, open deliberation and, most of all, concentration, to overcome the distrust that was injected into the slave culture.

Gatekeepers prove they don't know how to follow by having no plan to follow. They don't have a clue how to construct one and won't allow anyone to show them the ropes. Just because a person watches a jet airplane fly doesn't mean they know how to fly one. By the same token, just because highly educated "African Americans" who work in good-paying jobs parade as leaders and are seen in the company of white leaders doesn't mean he or she understands the basic fundamentals of leadership or has the mettle to follow another slave. In a competitive society like America, a leader must be able to see far enough ahead to envision what is going to happen based on what has already happened according to what is currently taking place.

If slave leaders can't rationalize to some degree what is going to take place in the near future, they won't be able to warn their followers of pitfalls ahead as leaders from other nationalities do. If leaders, no matter their nationality, don't have the aptitude to be farsighted, they *must* follow someone who is perceptive who knows the way; even if it means taking orders from someone with less *formal* education but who has reached the point where they understand the advancement process, can see pitfalls ahead and understands how to avoid disasters.

The seed is planted; help has arrived; let's get on with it!

Taking into account that the slave culture is America's only offspring and considering the circumstances surrounding slave descendants' racial birth, it's only poetic justice that American Slaves' ethnic birthday, or start of their *self-sufficiency,* be celebrated prior to when other cultures celebrate their American Independence Day. With these thoughts in mind and to make sure the slave culture would henceforth be correctly recognized by the appropriate authority and in the proper pecking order, slave descendants became a legally accepted part of America on July 3, 2001. This means Descendants of American Slaves racial independence is henceforth celebrated one day before America celebrates its Independence Day. Now slave descendants can do business legally out in the open and under their legitimate name: American Slaves, Inc.

OK, we're ready; who's going to lead us?

American Slaves, Inc. was formed and incorporated by a slave descendant who has a working knowledge of how America operates. Norris Shelton is fortunate and honored to be the founder and first president of American Slaves, Inc. That makes him the leader of a group of abandoned slaves who don't know who they are; therefore, they have no idea that he is even leading them.

At the appointed time, slave descendants will awaken, cultivate, take root and begin to grow. As change take place, they will take on an American flavor and begin to adjust to the ways of freedom. Slave descendants, like America, will select their leaders from the general population and elect their *one* leader diplomatically using the ballot.

Structuring a new breed of humans to be functional in a biased, commercial society hasn't been spelled out before. Since there are no known rules that explain how to start a human subculture or regulations in place describing how to breathe life into a group of abandoned slaves, ASI is afforded the opportunity of making up the rules as we move forward. Guiding principles that will control the organization will be based on what happened in the past, what is currently taking place and what we want to happen for slave descendants in the future. Realizing that leadership is slave descendants' weakest point, ASI will constantly seek premium leaders to succeed existing weaker leadership.

Once ASI starts holding elections, it will be up to succeeding leaders to sell their own plan of leadership to the slave culture before they can be voted in and be able to take the helm. ASI is structuring the slave culture in the same democratic manner that America, American Slaves' mother country, is structured.

In the past, "African Americans" became leaders of slave descendants by osmosis or by "hook-or-crook." They just wound up in the leadership slot and didn't even have an advancement plan that was designed to advance slaves — not even in their minds! Consequently, this time as we move forward, the joint leadership of the Slave Nation must be *carefully* thought-out and *well-planned*. Leaders at every level must have a diagram that points the way to true freedom that coincides with the master plan. Each diagram must be understood by all who are involved. When individual plans are accepted, leaders will be in charge of implementing their part of the plan and will be held accountable.

The leadership procedure for American Slaves will work the same way America's leadership process works when a candidate is running for President of The United States of America or other public office: A candidate is first selected because of his plan and then elected if he can sell his plan to the majority of the population. Once the majority buys the plan, the elected is allowed to select his cabinet and seek legislative approval.

Dr. King envisioned great possibilities for his people. He wound up in a leadership slot and he had a good idea where he was going. Unfortunately, he hadn't reached the point where he knew exactly how to get there. Therefore, he didn't have a plan and couldn't leave a written diagram for his people to follow after he was assassinated. Most Americans never did understand his true mission. When he tried to enlighten his followers of what it would take to make his dream come true, he was brutally murdered.

Most Americans praised him for his electrifying voice, strong delivery and for dreaming the impossible dream, which was equality for "Negroes." After reading between the lines in his book, *Why We Can't Wait,* we realize that, although he had a dream, his ultimate mission was to point descendants of slaves in the right direction! This tells us that Dr. King might have had a plan after all. It could have been in his book — *hidden between the lines!* That's why slave descendants must start reading! He told his followers plainly that their next challenge would be on the "economic battlefield," which is the business arena! Since ASI is a leadership unit and headed up by business minds, it became ASI's duty to study Dr. King's work until we understood what the words "economic battlefield" meant. To build on what Dr. King started, we not only had to read — we had to learn how to think so we would understand what Dr. King was planning *in his mind* to do!

After Dr. King was assassinated, inadequate leaders took the helm and seemingly forgot all about the "economic battlefield." In a state of confusion, they changed slave descendants' name from "Negro" to "African American." Misnomers caused slave descendants to veer farther off course. Now they are lost, confused and alienated, wandering aimlessly without direction still following the same type of backward leaders that got them lost.

Confused slave descendants following lost "African American" leaders in search of an illusionary "economic battlefield" illustrate the ignorance in the slave culture and why it exists. Only a business mind that relies on firsthand intelligence relevant to commerce could lead slave descendants into the 'jungle of business' and succeed in an economic struggle.

We can't afford to wait any longer!

Our current President's platform coming into office was to build on the words Dr. King spoke to America. Being an industrialist, he believes the two most important words Dr. King uttered to his followers were: "economic battlefield." Therefore, ASI's President's mission became to jump-start the American Slave Nation, turn the people around and head them in the right direction: towards the "economic battlefield." His duties include: properly identifying the people, legalizing their actions, mobilizing the American Slave Movement and then documenting slave descendants' advancement into mainstream America accordingly. His main assignment is to log the information he gathered while in business in "hardcopy" so it will live on in "book-form" and bring about forward thinking perpetually and ongoing positive change. He is sworn to act according to his writings. The information in this book is another reason why slave descendants must get into the habit of reading: Their leader, the President of American Slaves, Inc., is pointing out barriers that stand in their way and supplying them with written instructions that will show them how to advance on the "economic battlefield!"

To move a people forward in a commercial setting, a written plan is essential. That's why, for years, our president studied American Slaves' situation and collected information he judged would be needed to build a slavery foundation strong enough to support future advancement for a group of people who were bred to be unaware. After compiling data, he wrote what might be termed the "American Slave Bible." He called his publication: *America's Little Black Book.*

To give another illustration of how the gatekeeper system works, when *America's Little Black Book* was introduced to highly educated "African Americans," they said the findings were unsubstantiated and the work was unacceptable. This is a diversionary tactic that is subconsciously taught to "African American" gatekeepers in schools of higher learning.

You would normally expect bigoted whites to quote phrases like this. A slave descendant at the bottom of the barrel who is ignorant, yet knows his people need help — substantiated or unsubstantiated — wouldn't say something as backwards as *unsubstantiated,* especially when he has no other leads or ideas of his own!

If educators had been doing their jobs, they would have come to this knowledge long before it was figured out by grassroots slaves. Smart leaders would never suppress vital knowledge that could help their people advance no matter who presented it; especially when the knowledge is uncovered and presented to them on a silver platter! Given time, innovative knowledge and accumulated intelligence will *substantiate* itself. In the meantime, we must rely on common sense.

Realizing the *unsubstantiated* roadblock would undoubtedly raise its ugly head again in the future, the president of American Slaves, Inc. had to drop what he was doing and spend several more years writing additional books to explain why he, a businessman, was taking a *commercial approach* to guide slaves descendants, a product of commercial America, into mainstream America — *a commercial country!*

The effort unaware "African Americans" waste trying to make ASI substantiate findings that are intentionally covered up would be better spent helping ASI help their people. Gatekeepers, having no idea how to move the slave culture forward use big words like *unsubstantiated* to hide their failings and block ordinary slave descendants from advancing past them. They heard whites using big words like this in the front office, so they figure the words must be right. They fail to realize the damage a *single* word can do to a group of ignorant people in a legalized, paperwork society. The front office was put in place during slavery by educated people; some who helped baptized American Slaves in ignorance. Words that could help slaves weren't considered in the lingo then and they still aren't.

Most Americans, not understanding nation building or that America is a commercial country, will assume that a leader of slaves, according to leadership standards, would fritter away his time raising funds, explaining why his methods aren't working or seeking reelection to his or her office. Ordinarily, a leader's function is to stay in the eye of the public reciting speeches someone else wrote, not shut up in a room writing for so many years. The president of ASI realizes that to build a nation you must first lay down a solid foundation. His writings portray what he has seen in America with his own two eyes. They clarify, from a sensible perspective, why a plan is needed, what it takes to initiate the plan and what a suitable plan will accomplish long-term for America at large. What he witnessed has already allowed him to write a beginning plan. The outcome of his insight will become the cement that will hold the foundation of the slave culture together.

To see the devastation caused by "Negroes" not having a continuation plan to follow and adequate leadership to point the way after Dr. King was assassinated, ASI compared the lack of progress of slave descendant to the swift advancement other cultures have made that have come into America since the "Negro" Civil Rights Movement fell apart. Clearly, the slave culture is nearing disaster stage. If drastic steps aren't taken, slave descendants could wind up beyond repair. They have already fallen too far behind to be considered a top contender in today's economy. Not having a plan to follow and a *smart* leader to lead the way set the slave culture back at least 100 years! Slave descendants should never allow their culture to be caught without adequate leadership or an understandable advancement plan, ever again. Therefore, the main job of the president of ASI, at this juncture, is to draw up a *written continuance plan* how to expedite slave descendants moving forward, so the slave culture will have specific instructions to guide them after he steps down.

Needed: Salesman of the Millennium

During slavery, when slaves were sold at auctions, the auctioneer would highlight the slaves' attributes, brawn, intelligence or anything else he thought would sell his product, and business was good. To sell slavery back to today's fast-paced, misinformed American public with the same fervor, the threat of rectifying slavery must be removed and any benefits that could be derived from the proper rectification of slavery must be brought to light. The idea is to make all Americans feel good about the rectification of slavery. The sales pitch must be upbeat and bubbling with pride. This means pride in America, which slave descendants don't have at the moment, must be found or either created and it must be authentic.

It should be obvious to all why slave descendants aren't proud of America; nevertheless, because of bigoted repercussion, it's best not to say out loud that slaves aren't proud of their motherland. Our First Lady, Michelle Obama, told America that, until her husband was nominated to become the first black President of The United States of America, she hadn't had pride in America. The news media homed in on that statement and tried to make the simple truth spoken to unaware listeners by an honest lady sound like an all-out conspiracy against America. ASI applauded her, and America should have thanked her. She was supplying us with valuable information. America needs to know how the people really feel about conditions in our homeland, past and present. It's unfortunate that bigots don't want to hear the barefaced truth.

Mrs. Obama, even in her highly respected position, had to hurriedly resort to double-talk and change that tune before her husband was allowed to enter the White House as our Commander and Chief. This tells us that, even when American Slaves speak the truth, they still aren't allowed "free speech" without repercussion, unless they're saying what bigoted whites want to hear. Slave descendants would like to be proud of America and respect lawmakers, but pride and respect has to be earned.

Removing the shame of slavery from the heartbeat of the Slave Nation and introducing the self-importance of slave descendants to those who have been misinformed will take some of the negativity out of human bondage. One *huge* point of pride is the First lady of America is a Descendant of American Slaves — *and so are her children!* She is in the perfect position to help her people and, thankfully, she already has a copy of *America's Little*

Black Book. Hopefully, she has had a chance to read it.

If we look at slavery from a business point of view and then take into consideration that the breeding of slaves was necessary to the building of America, American Slaves should be allowed the opportunity to compete for America's wealth and excel in America the same as immigrant cultures excel. That within itself is a prideful statement. If it were a reality, it could be the motivating force that seals the freedom deal. With this thought in mind, whoever is selling slavery to "African American" leaders should always stress that the consequences of slavery aren't all bad. Without slavery, slave descendants wouldn't have been born in America. This glorious opportunity that's staring America's only offspring in the face wouldn't be at hand.

If gatekeepers were to step aside and allow astute leadership to takeover and lead or if they would help ASI sell slavery back to America, slave descendants would at least have a *chance* at having a bright future. The beauty of looking at slavery in an entirely different light is that it can now be easily rectified in slave descendants' favor but it will still benefit whites.

That's exciting stuff! It's a win/win proposition! Slavery will always be one of the foremost building blocks in the foundation of America. Therefore, the simple truth, even though it's hundreds of years old, becomes a fresh new approach. Another positive: America couldn't have been built and wouldn't have evolved as it did if not for slavery. That's a grateful acknowledgement! It makes slavery and American Slaves' factual identity the bond that solidifies the Slave Nation and stabilizes America. The idea of this sales approach is to use truth, racial importance, human sacrifice, impending potential and good intentions as the main selling points. It's foolish for slave descendants to be ashamed that they are the product of slavery and that their culture was produced by *corporate America.* American Slaves are the only group of people on the face of this earth who are totally American made! *America produced a superior product!* That's total pride! The product might *appear* inferior, but only because it hasn't been developed yet; we're just now starting the development process.

Slave descendants must start doing prideful things in honor of their culture. How can they expect whites and other nationalities to be proud of them if they are not proud of themselves? Staying angry about slavery, impersonating foreigners and acting out their frustrations because they are descended from slaves is getting the slave culture nowhere! It is up to slave descendants, the only begotten, to prove that America truly is the land of opportunity. They must learn to cherish their beginning and own up to their earthly existence.

Many whites gave their lives just so American Slaves could have this golden opportunity. American Slaves don't realize it but they owe the white culture a huge debt of gratitude. Imagine what would happen if slave descendants were to start showing favor to whites for delivering them from slavery. At least it would be something different. Keep in mind, President Obama said: "It's time for change we can believe in!" It's up to American Slaves to make change happen. They are a unique group of American citizens that were bred by whites whose time has come. It's only because of weak leadership that their destiny is still unclear.

ASI believes in America; it is our homeland and, for that reason, ASI is operating under the assumption that America is a benevolent society. This means American Saves still have an excellent chance of reaching their fullest potential and enjoying a bright future, but we have a question. Why didn't *benevolent* America deliver the slave culture out of the rut slave descendants find themselves in? Was it fear, malice or just neglect?

After thinking about slave descendants' situation, which is covert stagnation in the midst of America's abundant affluence, which are wealth, power and goodwill, it was concluded that slave descendants' racial stagnation was caused by all three, but ignorance fueled by greed and hate had to be the deciding factor. Why else would a beautiful country like America allow a blemish to fester in her fabric for so long — *unless this great nation is simply ignorant of how to rectify the situation?* It doesn't make sense.

Once it was concluded that ignorance was the snag that was holding the slave culture in mental bondage, our next objective became to unravel the mystery of why those blacks who claim to be leaders accept slave descendants' destitute condition as the norm, knowing American Slaves were bred in America for commercial purposes only and that their descendants still reside in the wealthiest country in the world. You would think at least one "African American" leader or black institution that represent coloreds, "Negroes" and "African Americans" would *at some point* realize Descendants of American Slaves' proper identity — it's their job! It is now suspected that racial ignorance in America is spread across the board, encompassing not only American Slaves but the white race and other nationalities as well — because the job is not getting done!

It's hard to believe that American Slaves, Inc. is the only organization in America that knows who slave descendants are and the ramifications of their being born slaves in a commercial society that boasts freedom for all. Maybe ASI is the only organization that is not too ashamed to acknowledge facts and has the nerve to speak the awful truth.

To make sure ASI wasn't alone in our effort to rectify slavery, we first concentrated on contacting those who we thought were the leaders of slave descendants — and were we in for a surprise. ASI hadn't counted on so much resistance from the very people we were trying to help. It became plainly obvious that "African American" leaders *at every level* have no idea who slave descendants are. Then we found out they didn't even understand the basics of freedom in a commercial country. That's why slave descendants are stuck in a slavery mode and why gatekeepers so readily accept being Uncle Toms. Confused leaders don't have a clue how to secure true freedom for their people in a business-driven environment; therefore, they fend only for themselves. Conversely, ignorant followers have no idea how to hold inadequate leaders accountable; therefore, they just follow along behind lost leaders who are not leading them; nearsighted leaders don't even recognize them.

When whites chastise "African American" leaders for doing a lousy job fending for their people and for dumping on their own kind, weak leaders go into a pitiful mode and seek racial sympathy and, right on cue, tenderhearted slave descendants go into a compassionate mode and rush to Uncle Tom's rescue. Slave descendants have actually been known to attacked whites for trying to help them advance and have unknowingly applauded "African American" leaders for their blundering failures.

Long-lasting freedom for slaves who were kept ignorant intentionally and that condition intended to perpetuate has never been defined or spelled out before. Since no one really knows the full extent of the cerebral damage that was done to American Slaves, those who truly care are at a loss to know what true freedom for Descendants of American Slaves should consist of.

American Slaves, Inc. has published various books that examine why the slave culture is pulling up the rear behind other American cultures in economics and what to do to improve slave descendants' situation. The books are: *America's Little Black Book* (To awaken the people and be their guide as they prepare to enter mainstream America); *Alley Rat* (To show the lowest of slaves that no matter where they started from — the cotton fields of Tallapoosa, Georgia — the bottom of the barrel in Eddy Alley — the jailbird or the derelict hanging on the street corner — if they put forth the necessary effort they can still succeed in life); *Crabs In A Barrel* (To illustrate the many ways that slave descendants as a people hold each other back by refusing to work together for the common good); *Black Name, White Game* (To show descendants of slaves how to pick themselves up when they get knocked down and how the American Slave movement got started and, most recently, *American Slaves, Inc. Renaissance Plan: The Next Step Forward* (the long overdue plan or vehicle that explains how slave descendants can enter mainstream of America).

All books, including this one, were written to support the proposition that dark-skinned Africans were extracted from Africa, transported to America and then *selectively* bred for servitude. *America's Little Black*

Book explains that during the breeding process, a premeditated mental transformation took place within this group of people on American soil. Therefore, when offspring came forward into the world, they were no longer captured Africans. The essence of their tribal being was born in America. Their ethnic mentally or outlook on life was created on American soil; therefore, they came forth as — *American Slaves* — not Africans, or African slaves! Descendants of American Slaves are not "African Americans" and they never were! This terminology wasn't even around during slavery when slaves were bred; therefore, it was never intended to be included in American Slaves' framework. These two words, "African *and* American," represent two entirely different countries. When used jointly, they are too impacting to be used to identify an American people without a *clear* understanding of why they are being used simultaneously and in chorus.

Slave descendants accepted the handle "African American" because a majority of them have slightly darker skin-tone than the average person from other American cultures. Slaves have gone along with the "African American" charade because no on has told them that skin-tone is not the only factor to consider when determining a person's nationality. In view of the wide variety of skin-tones in the slave culture, their leaders should already know this. It's widely known that all humanity sprang from Africa; therefore, every culture has roots in Africa. If other nationalities thought claiming their African roots would help them in America's business competition, they would probably all claim they were "Africans Americans" too, and for good reason: the acquisition of wealth. American Slaves must grow up and move on as other cultures did.

Diverse cultures, including Africans, are rushing into America staking a claim on America's wealth. American Slaves is the *only* ethnic group that has a legal, moral right to a claim — yet they are denying their true slave heritage while clinging to poverty and claiming to be Africans, merely immigrants! So, please — listen up, leaders — stop using misnomers to identify an American people who are being abused simply because they are ignorant of their proper identity. They were improperly identified by a biased, non-caring system. These people need help! To render aide to people who don't know who they are, you must first get their attention — *call them by their proper name* — they will answer! Generic, carefully constructed speeches delivered to a wrongly identified, unaware people, by backward "African American" leaders, do more harm than good.

Raise your children (the young slave nation) right, today, mother America, or suffer the consequences tomorrow

Commercial success in America does not happen automatically; therefore, children are taught early in life how to succeed. Paralleling a single child to a young inexperienced group of people tells us that American Slaves must be properly prepared to succeed in America's business environment just as white children are properly prepared to have a prosperous life in America. White children receives proper tutoring in the home, school, church, etc. Slave descendants live in a society where differing cultures compete for group-wealth; therefore, American Slaves, as a group, must be taught in the home, school and church, etc. how to compete in American commerce. Whites realized that commercial success doesn't just happen when they started America; that's why they bred slaves: to help them acquire wealth. Now it's time for whites to help slaves get mentally free and help them acquire wealth.

In order for the white culture to help slave descendants become financially free, white decision makers must have a clear understanding of slave descendants' present plight, their potential and their future intention. Therefore, a freedom plan must be developed, refined, and ultimately sold to the governing body of America. Whoever is gathering evidence and assembling the sales packet should focus on the illegal breeding of slaves — *not as individuals* — but as a subculture! Sure there are a few affluent "African Americans" in America. That's not what ASI is dealing with. Our effort is to systematically uplift the *Slave Nation* as a whole and in a peaceful manner. This might not sit too well with the weaker Uncle Toms, but those who are astute shouldn't despair; "the cream will still rise to the top."

Sticking points that must be considered and changed into selling points are that American Slaves were abandoned in a highly competitive business environment and left there to compete against the masters who bred and enslaved them for their survival. The stickiest point of all is that slave descendants are still unaware in the commercial country where they were bred where intelligence is the lifeblood. It all boils down to the long-lasting, deep-rooted ignorance slave descendants inherited. It's the most crushing problem of all and could wind up being "the kicker!" Because of this stubborn ignorance, too many slave descendants depend on inadequate welfare for their source of income. In an industrial society, handouts are not the answer; it destroys the aggression needed to compete so they can survive.

The guidelines that outline freedom for slaves must be debated by those who oppose slavery but who understand how freedom is obtained in a commercial country. Once the guiding principles are agreed upon, refined by the group and then presented to the governing body, acceptance should be in the offing. For the first time in the history of America, American Slaves will have a legitimate paper trail and be in a position to present their case to the proper authorities and to America at large. If enough data is compiled and "African American" leaders start doing their jobs and the American voters say so, reparations for slavery will get on the ballot. This would allow the American population to choose slave descendants' recompense and their future by way of vote.

Because of ignorance, shame, blatant stupidity and a lack of common sense, the guidelines that outline true freedom for slave descendants cannot be prepared by current "African American" leadership unless a mental transformation takes place first. Having allowed themselves to be bought off with trinkets, pacified with token titles and placated by being permitted to occasionally bask in the public spotlight, clearly shows they don't understand the fine art of negotiation. They blew it when they were negotiating "minority programs." American Slaves had better get it right this time. We may never get this chance again. ❖

4

Correcting the
Slave Mentality
(Willie's prediction: The slave
mentality will last for 300 years)

(KPE) knowledge, planning and execution

One word that gatekeepers rely on is "security." This term has "African American" leaders all screwed up. Whites have been waving this word in front of slave descendants ever since the Civil War ended. "African American" leaders assume as long as they keep their heads down, protect what is theirs and don't take chances or make waves, they'll be secure like whites are. This is a misleading notion because whites are being led by astute leaders and whites understand how to follow. Slave descendants aren't being led at all and, having no idea how to follow, they just tag along behind the crowd. Following blindly does not lead to security. Racial pressure is steadily building in America. Slave descendants have started killing each other at an alarming rate, and there is no plan in place how to put an end to this senseless slaughter — *except one:* the *American Slaves, Inc. Renaissance Plan!* American Slaves must acquire leaders with the intelligence and courage to tell unaware stragglers, who are restless and growing up wild, the truth of why they are behind and then teach them how to catch-up!

Until the slave culture is given accurate information, they will stay lost and confused and, because they are frustrated, they will keep right on killing each other out of frustration. If slave leaders don't start acting like they've got some sense and accept the only plan that outlines how their followers will *at least* have a chance to catch up to immigrant cultures, no slave descendant can be secure — simply because America can't be secure. At this point, grassroots slave descendant don't even try to be secure. They know from experience that no matter the situation they don't have a chance to win, anyway. They figure "what the hell's the use in even trying." That's the wide ranging attitude among most American Slaves — and it's defensible!

In an industrial society that boasts freedom for all, fairness is the mother of security. Racial well-being grows into a healthy product when people work together for a common cause. Security is nurtured with knowledge and cultivated with hope. This means that anything other cultures can do — slave descendants *should* be able to do too; which in their case is not true. Leaders must study the past to understand what transpired during slavery that stops Descendants of American Slaves from progressing like other cultures progress. Knowledge is the key to cultural development in a moneymaking environment. The rest is planning, hard work and execution but the main ingredient is still hope. ASI repeats: Without hope, there is no honest exertion.

Illuminating the security myth

ASI is breaking new ground so, as we go forward, we must always be keenly aware that we are leading a group of unaware people who are held in a deliberately planned unconscious state and, as Willie Lynch predicted, someday they will awaken. This means we must make haste because, at some point, their eyes will come open and they will see and understand the devastation whites caused to the slave culture. To avoid upheaval in the future, ASI's main job is to make waves today! We must plan ahead so the awakening of the American Slave Nation won't be a hostile beginning. That's why ASI has worked hard so many years to come up with the *American Slaves Renaissance Plan*. It is beneficial to all Americans. It generates love for mankind, hope for the future and respect for all human form.

To overcome inertia and move forward in a business setting, slave descendants must keep the six P's of business at the forefront of their way of thinking: "Proper Planning Prevents Piss Poor Performance." Proper planning is the mother of proper execution. *America's Little Black Book* gives us the key to success: "KPE," (Knowledge, Planning and Execution). If understood, the information in the book will lead slave descendants in the direction of security. It is left to those who have the mettle to lead a group of abandoned slaves to come up with a viable plan and then teach the slave culture how to execute it properly so they can reach their planned goal.

The single most important rule that controls a business society where residing cultures compete is to make money *collectively*. The slave culture is impoverished because, as a people, slaves absolutely refuse to work collectively unless whites are in charge. Slaves think they are working together, independent of whites, but they are not. The white culture has always been in charge. Their group is affluent because they believe in working together, no matter who's in charge, even if it's an American Slave and the consequences are obvious.

Now that we have explored the problems that slave descendants are faced with, before we move forward, let us look back at what we have to work with: Number one: Slaves were bred in America which was an immoral act sanctioned by white Americans the dominant culture. Number two: Slavery was a *legal* business enterprise and recognized as such by America's "powers that be." Number three: Slavery was ultimately judged to be illegal and immoral. That's the chief reason why the Civil War was fought and why white people killed each other — but that's not the full account of human bondage. There are other pieces of the slavery puzzle that must be taken into considerations: America is a commercial society that is controlled by legalities and strict guidelines. Even though the white culture is the dominant culture and can do pretty much whatever they want to do, they didn't just wake up one morning and start killing each other because the North hated the South nor because either locale loved slaves. The North and South were involved in fierce economic competition that would shape

America for the future. To gain an advantage, the South started mass-breeding slaves right out in the open. Profits from slavery allowed the South to rise in prominence. However, the illegal act of slavery prompted the North to fight the South until they unchained their slaves. That's not the end of the slavery story either; because slave descendants survived and America is still ongoing — therefore, the story continues

Legal paperwork compiled by an unscrupulous social order

Organizing the Civil War and strategizing the outcome of the most *violent* part of America's recorded history was by no means taken lightly. It doesn't matter that the event was misunderstood or whether America realized it or not, or didn't recorded it *accurately* or not — *the American Slave culture was still being born!* Without even knowing it, God's Will was being carried out. America made quite a racket introducing those four million slaves to the world! Many meetings took place; mounds of legal documents were signed, compiled, catalogued and stored; bombs were bursting in the air; people as well as animals were angry, confused and frightened, running in all directions, screaming for help and dying by the thousands. The pain from birth was unbearable, and *Mother America was screaming out from the top of her voice!* American Slaves were coming forth — being delivered on American soil and the South was the "delivery-room."

Another point to keep in mind is that America didn't issue birth certificates to slaves because America really didn't understand what was happening. At that time, it was documented *in writing* and accepted by the Government that those four million slaves being born (turned out into the world) were animals, merely livestock — or were they? What became of the paperwork and other documents that declared slaves were animals before the war began. Better yet, what became of the documents that declared slaves were human and not animals after the war was over?

If no paperwork is found to specify otherwise, we must ask ourselves are slaves still classified as animals, legally. Could it be that slave descendants are still classified as livestock by law but don't know it? When were they unclassified as animals and reinstated into the human race?

Freedom in a commercial society is not a routine thing. It must be supported by an insightful paper trail. Therefore, we must ask ourselves if American slaves were really freed. Where are the files that verified that American Slaves were properly freed and remunerated for services rendered during slavery? After all, isn't that's what the war was supposed to be all about, freeing the slaves because slavery was morally wrong and then found to be illegal? In a free society, it's unlawful to force people to work. Not paying them for their forced labor just compounds the crime.

It's immoral and completely thoughtless for America to turn ignorant slaves *that she bred* out into a commercial society that's filled with hostile immigrants without any protection or means of survival. Forcing them to compete against their enslavers for their continued existence in the country *they helped build* is cruel and merciless. Then having the cowardice to call *expulsion* from slavery freedom is clearly sadistic. When it all boils down and the absolute truth is told, the War was fought to free slaves but American Slaves weren't given any consideration at all. The Civil War was nothing more than an economic struggle that involved the business of slavery.

Instead of being set free properly, which would have included monetary compensation, a mental upgrade and their freedom clearly defined, slaves, born on American soil, yet poverty-stricken and totally unaware of economics, were released from slavery and dumped into a cold-blooded business environment without guidance or any offer of stewardship whatsoever. Newly freed slaves didn't know how to think — thinking had always been the master's job. If the mentality of American Slaves hadn't been damaged and they understood how to rationalize correctly, they would have realized right away that the Civil War wasn't about their freedom at all. The War was about slavery — *and slavery was business!* Therefore, the Civil War was simply a war machine for accomplishing an end — just another tactic whites use to "take care of business."

Slaves need a leader who understands the thinking process

When Dr. King fell, the slave culture wound up with no leadership. Without a standing leader to issue orders or tell the remaining leaders what to do so they could tell the people what to do, inactivity set in. Void of thinking power and precise rationalization, "Negroes," not knowing what to do or which way to go, became stuck. If "Negro" leaders hadn't been frightened of ending up like Dr. King, gunned down in the street, they would have studied the leadership tactics he employed in the Civil Rights movement and used the same principles he used to keep the people moving forward. Filled with fright and void of advancement know-how, "Negro" leaders took the safe-way out. They stayed in the public eye as leaders alright, but their leadership tactics and advancement schedule dwindled to grieving over Dr. King's death and participating in mournful dedications to celebrate his birthday. "African Americans" still think celebrating the rise and fall of their "Negro" leader is moving forward!

Instead of ASI mourning Dr. King's death and celebrating his birthday, we decided to commemorate his life by moving away from slavery towards freedom in the direction he told "Negroes" to go when he was alive. He told his followers in simple language to head for the economic battlefield. Granted that's not much information for ignorant slaves fresh out of slavery to go on but, coming from such a distinguished leader, it should have been enough to prompt some type of action. ASI got busy figuring out what moves a group of abandoned slaves would have to make to secure economical freedom in a biased business setting. We just took into consideration that American Slaves were mercilessly handicapped from the very beginning and how that handicap still affects slave descendants' advancement today.

The truth and nothing but the truth

At this juncture, slave descendants are caught-up in a paradoxical situation. "African American" leaders actually have the authority to advance the slave culture into mainstream America. The paradox occurs because they also have the power to stifle slave descendants' very existence and, knowingly or unknowingly, that's exactly what they're doing. If "African American" leaders really want to help their people achieve a measure of momentum, all they would need to do is follow counseling given them by American Slaves, Inc. If, on the other hand, the Willie Lynch syndrome has hardened their state of mind to the point they have a problem collaborating with the only organization that represents their true culture, all they would need to do is *reinterpret* the guidance given them by their current employers and act on those orders in their own peoples' behalf.

It does no good for ordinary slave descendants to tell white authority figures the truth about their dire condition. Even if whites wanted to help, they couldn't because they would have to call slave descendants by their accurately identifying name. Can you imagine what would happen if a white diplomat or a white person running for political office were to call a wannabe "African American" a slave or a slave descendant to his face? He would be committing political suicide or worse! Yet it's the only way whites could ever help the slave culture through this phase of their identity crisis — *they must call Descendants of American Slaves by their proper name!* The pieces will then fall neatly into place.

Whites know slave descendants need help. That's why they keep coming up with so many plans how to help American Slaves, except they call them *minority programs*. Calling slave programs minority programs allows white women, minority groups and every individual that has come into America, legally and illegally, to pillage every program designed to help slave descendants. Normally, by the time slave descendants learn about generic help programs, most of the funds have been commandeered by immigrants, foreigners and whites who understand the program better than unaware slaves do.

The slave culture has slowed to a standstill because weak leaders allowed American Slaves to be misidentified. Then they allowed every program designed to help slave descendants advance to be misnamed! If whites were to call minority programs what they should be called, which is "American Slaves Programs" instead of what sounds catchy to unaware slave descendants, "African American" leaders would attack in full force and grassroots slaves would support the assault.

Slave descendants are letting America off the hook for slavery today just like the North let the South off the hook for proper restitution to American Slaves for slavery after the Civil War. Proclaiming they are "African Americans" gives America the perfect excuse to keep turning a deaf ear to the slave culture and the needs an abandoned people.

Association brings about assimilation

A major hindrance in slave descendants advancing is they don't understand how to strategize collectively. Without collaborative information, they don't have sufficient data to parallel the many diverse cultures in America so they can see flaws within their own group. Understanding how other cultures progress is the only way American Slaves can understand how to construct a plan that will move impediments out of their way so their racial growth can begin in earnest.

The good news is slave descendants don't have to reinvent the wheel in order to construct a development plan that will move their group forward. All slave leaders would need to do is concentrate on the advancement techniques competing cultures have used to get ahead of American Slaves in their own country and do what other cultures normally do in a business setting and in their daily lives — the trick is to use whatever proceeds can be derived from slavery to do it better!

Most slave descendants don't understand the planning process. They don't seem to realize that they live in a business setting or what that truly means. That's why they seem so detached and incoherent to whites and those of us who understand business. Slave descendants don't spend their quality time doing business and discussing advancement techniques like individuals from other cultures do. It would never cross the average slave's mind to focus on a how to excel in a business setting.

Thinking is the name of the American business game but, because of the lack of association with businesspersons, the average slave hasn't learned how to think commercially. Slave descendants think on a personal, individual level because they have always been a divided people. Their leaders must start learning to think on a business level so they teach their followers how it's done. The reason why slaves are in a depressed non-thinking mode and don't understand business goes right back to inadequate leadership. The slave culture is not represented in corporate America because their business leaders aren't doing their jobs. There is however an explanation why slave businesspersons fall short: They have never had advancement options or a racial business plan, nor business avenues available to them that was designed to uplift a culture that was intentionally depressed. That's why ASI developed the "Renaissance Plan."

The average slave descendant actually think they are thinking how to get ahead in life when they reminisce about petty, meaningless things that aren't business related that add up to nothing more than stagnation. Unconscious procrastination keeps slave descendants at a standstill or either headed in the same erroneous direction. Too many slave descendants struggle just to stay alive. Many burn up their energy surviving drive-by shootings and other everyday dangers. A normal day for a lot of black people is spent concentrating on how to evade the law, collect welfare, stay one jump ahead of the system and stay out of jail. These traits are the exact opposite of what Dr. King saw in his dream.

ASI believes in America. It is our homeland and, for that reason, ASI is operating under the assumption that America is a benevolent society. This means American Slaves still have an excellent chance of reaching their fullest potential and enjoying a bright future.

While these behavior patterns might seem helter-skelter in some neighborhoods and to other cultures, existing in stagnation, mayhem and harmful peculiarities is routine in the 'hood; nothing more than everyday life for a majority of slave descendants. The power of assimilation has taken place and imbedded ignorance has taken its toll, and that's exactly what "Willie Lynch" was selling to slave owners in the year 1712.

According to slave status, ASI's president was successful in the business arena, and he did what other black leaders usually do when they become, what we in the 'hood call, "nigger-rich;" he relocated to the suburbs. Fortunately, he missed living among his own people and, after realizing that living upscale among other cultures that looked down on his people was highly overrated, he moved back into his old neighborhood. He soon saw that not too much had changed since he left; except *negative* assimilation had taken over. Or should we say it had stayed firmly in place.

Working closely with whites for a number of years, he had adapted to their way of life. White leaders insist on positive change and they work toward a pre-planned goal continually. They focus, and they work *closely* together. Comparing black leadership to white leadership, he began to understand adaptation and assimilation— *they have two sides* — good and bad! ASI's President was raised in Eddy Alley, clearly the bottom of the barrel and not something a person who has seen better would ordinarily want to adapt or assimilate to.

Once ASI's president was in a business setting, it was like "throwing the rabbit into the briar patch." Working closely with whites, he found himself right at home. In this case, because America is a corporation founded on business, assimilation is *very* good. What he learned in business, dealing with unscrupulous gatekeepers, white and black, couldn't be taken away because beneficial assimilation had taken place. He therefore made himself a promise: He would use what he learned in industry to help *all* of his people prosper instead of just the people he had been trying to help who he *thought* were dedicated leaders. Working with white leaders and scrutinizing their actions, he found out that black leaders weren't really leaders at all. They were in fact just scared Uncle Toms guarding the gate to opportunity and, just like they dumped on him, they were dumping on the rest of their people, also.

Considering what he learned in industry dealing with white and immigrant leaders, compared to what he was currently witnessing in the 'hood, he knew for certain negative adaptation had taken place and stagnation had a firm grip on "African American" leaders. Somehow, change had to take place. After meeting with existing leaders and analyzing their responses to his proposal to rectify slavery, he knew in their condition they wouldn't be of much help. Until they could understand to some degree some of the things he learned in industry and realize he was trying to help them, he would have to be the one to initiate change. Luckily, he has a decided advantage: his own gatekeeper-training.

Some might ask what is the differenence between the training Mr. Shelton recieved and the guidance other well-known, more educated gatekeepers received. Good question: Educated "African Americans" are in most cases shown only one side of American life according to what whites want them to see, and that's always predicated on what's best for whites. Gatekeepers are rarely shown the real side of commercial American. Therefore, they don't have a clue how groups of people can excel in industry once they learn how to work together. Uncle Toms have always been highly trained to function in only a certain area of endeavor according to the master's needs and always to the master's advantage. It should be obvious to all why slaves weren't shown the money-making side of American life: *The master didn't want slaves to have his wealth — they were his wealth!*

The ASI president's education was dissimilar and, according to the unspoken rules that keep slave descendants divided, confused, mentally enslaved and impoverished, probably illegal: Whites went to the expense and trouble of training him to take the lead in making them money in a business venture that couldn't fail that they couldn't be seen working in. He became a *certified minority* and ran a "front company" for whites. He calls it "collusion on the rocks with a minority twist."

The white guys who were tutoring him were managers on the inside of a major corporation in control of a product that could be easily manufactured and then sold to the corporation they worked for and also marketed worldwide. ASI's president had to learn the parts of business they don't teach in school and build on it. When training was over — *as a certified minority* — all he had to do was walk proudly, look good, don't make waves and follow the orders the whites gave him and the money would roll in. He didn't have the intelligence, or maybe he just didn't take the time, to ask these white guys exactly what being a *certified minority* really meant. He was just pleased, proud and in a hurry to be one. Amazingly, because he was a minority *and had papers to prove it,* he was the answer to their needs. He, like current "African American" leaders, was completely unaware of what was going on around him and, just like today's titular leaders; he loved every minute of it. ASI's president actually thought "minority" was his birthright! At the time, he simply didn't know any better: It's called ignorance.

Before whites thrust him into the manufacturing arena, they formed a legal corporation with him as president, not because he was descended from slaves (that was never even mentioned) and definitely not because he was qualified, because they knew he wasn't — *it was because he had been certified as a minority!* Despite the fact that he was under-educated, ill-prepared and, according to manufacturing standards, destitute, he still warned these whites that, because they were intercepting money that should rightfully go to his people, he would use whatever knowledge and wealth he gained in the scheme to "give back" to his people — *whom he thought were born minorities.*

Hearing this, they balked; explaining that everyone else was getting a piece of the minority action, so why shouldn't they. They had a point and realizing his back was against the wall, he knew if he wanted to play in their game, he would have to play by their rules; so he told them he wouldn't draw attention to the scheme. His promise of secrecy overrode the possibility that he might upset the applecart and, thinking they could change his mind about him helping his people, greed overrode caution and they welcomed him into the gatekeeper fraternity with open arms. Thus began his own gatekeeper experience, with one *huge* difference: He had full knowledge he was being trained to be a "money-making" Uncle Tom for these white guys.

With hindsight, he now realizes that succumbing to becoming an Uncle Tom was a great trade-off and the best thing he could have done in honor of his people. The "front company" theory *really* works! A program of this nature could become a valuable learning tool and a practical advancement vehicle for slave descendants. It could be their ticket to racial independence. Whites trained ASI's President how to do business in a white setting and he's using that training to help his people. Uncle Toms of today could do the same thing. They've already been trained and they're already in the right position. They could help their people and there would be no repercussions — they just don't realize it! If they were to use their acquired training to help their people, it would legitimize the gatekeeper position and give credibility to gatekeepers themselves.

The beginning of the American Slave culture could be similar to the beginning of Mr. Shelton's business career. ASI uses this parallel to assure the reader that if slave descendants are tutored properly, they can excel in business. We simply parallel what happened to a single slave, ASI's President, to what could happen to the slave culture in general if they learned to work together and were tutored properly. Whites programmed ASI's President for business while his mind was fresh in the area of commerce and not cluttered with the abuse that is normally heaped upon slave descendants who have struggled in business, been wounded and already failed. He was taught right up front that hard-core *selling* is the essence of doing shrewd business.

Unfortunately, selling also has its downside; it's called rejection. Being constantly turned away, denied and dejected by unsympathetic buyers are physiological negatives that provoke unhelpful emotions that are also unhealthy because they can have an adverse effect on the seller's mentality; plus it can leave an unpleasant aftereffect on the situation at hand and the product being sold. Not many people can maintain a positive attitude being told *no* continually — and slaves have always been told no — continually! Whites schooled Mr. Shelton on how to deal with failure as simply a way of doing "tough-minded business." When someone tells you no, they're just asking for more information: *So keep banging on the door!*

For instance, he parallels the "no sale" scenario to "African Americans" viewing slavery as a failed proposition. It adds up to the same thing. American Slaves have always viewed slavery as the most disgusting thing that ever happened in America — *but only because slave descendants feel they are the victims of slavery* — which could or could not be true; either way it's still a negative.

ASI says slave descendants are victims of slavery only as long as they claim that title and *they* stay in that position. *Slavery wasn't a failure!* No way! Look at America: We are the pinnacle of dominance; we're rich, beautiful, powerful and strong! This tells us that slavery in American was the climax of *all* successful business ventures! Slave Descendants must learn to use what they *think* is the failure of slavery as a stepping stone into the future: Learn from getting knocked down — then get up with a vengeance! The fight is just now getting started! This is only the first round. It's time for slave descendants to wake-up, stand-up, come together, *and start banging on the door!*

Slave mentality personified

Whites programmed the ASI president's mind for business by telling him many things that only white businessmen discuss among themselves. It was in their best interest to instill in him the real truth about how business is done in America because he was operating at the highest level representing a company they wanted to succeed worldwide. He was actually thrust into a position where he had to deal with some of the brightest white minds in the world and the crassest Uncle Toms in America while often shooting from the hip! The knowledge he received and the experience he gained helped level the business playing field. That information is not available to the slave culture because it can't be controlled by just whites alone. Just like slave masters placed ignorance at the root of the Slave Nation, and it grew; whites placed the truth of how business is really done in America at the root of the ASI president's industrial career, and from there his business mentality grew.

> *Slavery won't be straightened out overnight but we must start somewhere, someday to put an end to this degrading stagnation.*

"African American" leaders don't realize they are still taking their lead from slave masters. Not realizing their leaders are being led by the nose by American Slaves' worst enemy, grassroots slave descendants willingly take their cue from "African American" leaders. That's why Willie Lynch predicted his program would last for 300 years. On the other hand, slave descendants shouldn't rely solely on his prediction. Their imbedded ignorance and the damaged mentality their group inherited won't automatically come to an end in the year 2012, not if slave descendants keep reproducing in ignorance and continue evolving unaware of their true being. Slave descendants' intelligence won't improve unless they heed this information and *they themselves* initiate change.

Slavery won't be straightened out overnight but we must start somewhere, someday to put an end to this degrading stagnation. The more slave descendants are ignored, the more their mentality will erode. Where does it end, in total disaster? What will it take to get America's attention? What words will make leaders, white and black, understand that a dangerous situation is looming ahead and steadily growing? It's as plain as day — all they have to do is open their eyes!

During corporal slavery, there was a wide education gap between slave and master. Today, the education department is waving a big red flag *right in our faces* warning us that there is a *huge* education gap between slave descendants (aka "African Americans") and whites, but that's not the *core* of the fracture in America's foundation. There is a deeper over-riding gap between slave descendants and their Uncle Tom leaders.

Using comparisons to unearth a solution, we saw that during corporal slavery, withholding intelligence was the slave master's most effective weapon for keeping slaves ignorant and enslaved. The chains were removed, but it is now realized there were two sides to slavery that was carried out in America — physical and mental. Metal chains, brutality and ignorance held slaves captive then. Today, denying American Slaves their proper identity keeps slave descendants *mentally* enslaved.

Some argue that progress is being made. ASI counters that statement because it's not true. It's merely an illusion. Every time an educator, news-caster, preacher or anyone else in a position of authority or in the field of communication refers to slave descendants as "African Americans," they are instilling ignorance into *all* who hear, white and black, and therefore into the entire slave culture and America at large. That's not progress; that's perpetuating ignorance at the highest levels.

Spreading ignorance, even casually, might seem harmless but it's not because, at some point, the after effects of ignorance will surely surface. Slave descendants repeating words they heard white leaders and Uncle Toms spout, without understanding the ramifications of the words they are replicating, is ignorance in full bloom. When leaders get caught-up in saying the wrong thing, it influences those around them in a negative way and manipulates the actions of their followers. It could eventually lead to cultural collapse!

Without knowledge of the depraved process slave masters were us-ing to create slaves, the mental contamination that went into breeding the slave culture couldn't be discovered. Without *America's Little Black Book,* Descendants of American Slaves might never have become aware of what is happening to them. It's not practical for people who were bred to be ignorant, but don't know it, to search for a cure to an illness that purportedly doesn't even exist. Once ignorance has been injected into a group of human beings at the *root* of their existence and then given the necessary ingredient it needs to develop, which in American Slaves' case was repugnance for their own kind, it will carry forward for an extended time. If someone doesn't instigate a plan how to stop it, unless Divine intervention happens or a phenomenon takes place, it could harden and increase its stranglehold.

During slavery, few slaves were kept in chains unless they were being transported or disciplined. Typically, slaves stayed on the plantations did their chores and didn't cause trouble. This gives us clues as to how strong the slave mentality really is. Slaves knew they were being mistreated, and slave masters and owners knew they were heavily outnumbered by some of the most physically powerful people on earth. It's not normal for groups of physically stronger human beings to willingly accept servitude and abuse from a smaller force of individuals without some type of retribution — *unless special "mind-taming" has taken place.* This important evidence tells us that the mental bond of slavery was a lot stronger than the physical chains that everyone supposed were holding slaves captive. If it took an act of war to have the physical chains removed from slaves, yet the mental bond was actually stronger than the chains, what will it take to have slave descendants' mentality renovated and brought up to date — another war?

Gap Coordinators to the rescue

The Kentucky school system finally figured out that slave descendants' way of thinking wasn't improving and something had to be done, so they introduced Gap Coordinators. This gave us some hope but, after 18 years, the Board of Education released the horrifying news that Gap Coordinators had made every effort to close the education gap between "African Americans" and whites, but to no avail. That's why ASI got involved. Educators were overlooking the most important piece of evidence of all. It's not feasible to close a *racial* education gap without first considering and then understanding the ramifications of the word *race* — that's the first word you would stumble over. Slave descendants are not "African Americans!" *Our school system has simply targeted the wrong people!*

Before we get into exploring Gap Coordinators, let's consider that the bulk of American institutions, including the school systems, *claim* they don't discriminate. Why? Because everyone knows it is political suicide to discriminate by pointing out different cultures and branding them as inferior. Yet, the Kentucky Performance Report 2008 is doing *exactly* that — and getting away with it! Why? Because they know better than to call slave descendants by their accurately identifying name — which is *Descendants of American Slaves!* That one simple utterance, which is the *simple* truth, opens up a whole new "can of worms." It would surely blow the "cover-up" of slavery.

ASI is not registering a complaint by any means. In fact, we openly applaud the Kentucky school system for their effort and for sharing this extremely important information with us. It gave American Slaves, Inc. the opening we needed. For years we have been screaming that if slave descendants are to be helped — they must be singled out! How else could we ever hope to close the education gap that existed between slave and master then and still exists between whites and slave descendants today, unless we single out the victims of slavery by properly identifying them, legalizing them, stating the obvious to the proper authorities and then rendering suitable aid to the wounded, which in this case is the slave culture.

Leaders can't discuss slave descendants' factual situation and racial mental condition intelligently until they understand clearly who slave descendants are. They will never know who slave descendants are and why they are *slow* unless they know what slave masters injected into the core of their foreparents' mental composition. Leaders will never understand why slave descendants are actually self-destructing if "African American" leaders keep refusing to discuss the cause of the breakdown, which are the aftereffects of slavery.

Taking an even closer look

When all is said and done, there is no feasible plan being developed by current leaders, the board of education, our government, or anyone else to close the education gap that exists in Kentucky between slave descendants and whites. This gaping wound is not just in Kentucky. It's distributed *equally* throughout America. The reason why nothing is being done to alleviate this terrible setback is because no one is held accountable for slave descendants worsening condition. That's why the aftereffects of slavery are allowed to worsen in plain sight without hindrance.

ASI uses the Kentucky Performance Report 2008 as our barometer to understanding America's racial situation. It gives a clear picture that there are an inordinate number of slave descendant students, aka "African American" students, who remain in the achievement gap within Kentucky schools. The report, based on 100% learning capability, points out that "African American" children (slave descendants children), learn at a much slower pace than white children. The achievement gap, or children's ability to learn scale, is as follows:

	Whites	African Americans
Elementary	94.8	75.6
Middle School	89.1	67.1
High School	79.0	58.0

Now, keep in mind, it wasn't just white educators alone who supplied the information that was compiled in the Kentucky Performance Report. The data was put together by a variety of scholars who were familiar with researching projects of this nature. ASI would like to know how "African American" educators could stand idly by and allow this disgrace to continue for so many years. This dreadful condition goes straight to the heart of slave descendants' cultural difference. It controls their racial well-being. It's confusing that educators could compile an important *racial* report like this and completely overlook the obvious.

The report says loudly and clearly that, even though slavery has been over for more than a century and it's no longer against the law for slave descendants to be educated, something is still terribly wrong when it comes to their ability to learn — even when they are being taught in the same environment with whites! American Slaves, Inc. was commissioned to find out what is causing this vast difference. If learning disparity exists between whites and blacks in Kentucky schools at all levels and grades, unless Kentucky is in a class by itself, this difference exists to some degree in all public schools, nationwide.

Assuming all things were equal when the survey was taken, we must ask ourselves why, after better than *18 years,* our school system has made no headway in correcting this glaring deficiency. According to the report, *American Slaves are slowly easing backward!* If this much mental disparity exists in the American school system, wouldn't this give us clues as to why inequality exist in all facets of life between the white and slave cultures, nationwide? ASI desperately need slave descendants who are educators to lend a hand in this endeavor. It's really their job to take the lead in the proper education of their people but, for some reason they won't educate slave descendants properly, so ASI got involved.

We implore educators not to be afraid of losing job security or become offended to the point of not supporting our effort and shrink from doing their part in a timely fashion. "African American" leaders in the field of education already know their way around the education establishment. It's time they used their positions to help their own people by helping American Slaves, Inc. Some might ask why American Slaves, Inc. is venturing into the education arena. It's simple: Educators need help.

As the representative of Descendants of American Slaves, it's ASI's job to venture into all areas where there are slave descendants because there you will find discrimination and injustice. Our rescue effort must be comprehensive and reach across the board. Racial abuse in America is widespread and it has gone on long enough. Someone had to come up with some answers. ASI just stepped up to the plate — it's our turn at bat. *The Next Step Forward* was published for one purpose only: to help slave descendants understand how to advance from slavery into mainstream America.

ASI's *Renaissance Plan* was not drawn up to intimidate or belittle "African Americans." The word *renaissance* simply means revival or rebirth. The book validates the initial part of the American Slave Movement, an important, vigorous period of artistic and intellectual activity that slave descendants must go through. The plan outlines the rebirth and revival of the slave culture. It will help educators understand their *true* calling and enable them to get their jobs done better and more expeditiously.

In spite of educators saying they are doing everything they can to alleviate the learning disparity between blacks and whites, the education gap in Kentucky is well-documented. Hopefully, after reading this information, educators will realize they need help and have the good sense to accept it. Unless ASI is missing something here, the words Gap Coordinator signify that slave descendants' racial-failure is coordinated — *obviously by those in charge of coordinating the gap!* How else could the education gap that is summarized in the Kentucky Performance Report 2008 have remained consistent for so many years unless *carefully* coordinated?

Leaders in the field of education are paid good money to close education gaps but, unfortunately their effort is not producing any favorable results; unless doing nothing at all and then proudly publishing the disgraceful results is what educators consider favorable. Wouldn't our children have been better off if, for that past 20 years, Gap Coordinators had spent their time *closing* the education gap rather than just *coordinating* it?

Those who lead slave descendants must tell their people to start reading and they themselves must start reading; then they must understand what they read. Don't they realize that *not knowing how to read* was the strongest chain that held slaves captive? When slave leaders don't pay close attention to words and understand how and why they are used, they make stupid blunders. The words *Gap Coordinator* is the same type of double-talk as the words *Minority Program*.

"African American" leaders still haven't figured out the drawbacks of minority programs in regards to who slave descendants are in relation to their contribution to the building of America. Flawed programs only serve to keep the slave culture lagging behind other American cultures and fighting over the crumbs that fall from immigrants' tables. The words "African American" and *minority* have all but destroyed the slave culture, and now slave descendants are faced with trying to get past some of those same gatekeepers who initially started that non-thinking fallacy. "African American" leaders must start understanding the wording of documents and learn how to decode both legal and generic paperwork.

Slaves are behind; but the race just got underway

White Americans have no idea that they themselves are going through a bleak period of misconception. One major reason why ordinary blacks are looked down on is because "African American" leaders, trying to take the heat off themselves, have convinced whites that black, lowlife derelicts are to blame for the deteriorating condition of black neighborhoods. This is not even *close* to being true; in fact, it's a bald-faced lie! "African American" leaders are hurting their people a lot more than the ghetto thug that's wreaking havoc on black neighborhoods.

Slave descendants can overcome the thug waiting in the darkness to rob, pillage and openly kill them, individually, but cannot survive this most important stage of their growth if educators and other leaders in advancement positions keep screwing up and then hiding out and acting like they are innocent. They are not innocent! They're guilty! Ineffective leadership is silently killing the future of slave descendants' very existence by limiting the knowledge their children receive. That's the other side of slavery that leaders are overlooking and exactly how slave masters developed the slave mentality and installed it into their slaves without notice. Slave owners contaminated the mentality of Uncle Toms by tainting the information they received and then instructed them how to pass this ignorance on. Today, institutions taint data by omitting or either falsifying important information and then instructing highly educated gatekeepers how to pass on *well-worded* ignorance to unaware slave descendant children.

Without knowing the damage they are causing, gatekeepers and educators nurture ignorance and help it to perpetuate by discrediting anyone who tries to bring innovative intelligence to their attention. They think if someone points out ignorance they can't see, it belittles their intelligence, but it doesn't. It's difficult to help individual slave descendants who hold high-ranking positions. They insist on being political and using terminology that has little meaning. Most of them fail to realize that, when ASI singles them out as gatekeepers, we're only trying to help them realize what they've become. Ignorance disguised as political correctness allows inadequate leaders to keep right on being inadequate with the blessing of their people.

When dealing with a delicate subject like slavery and the ignorance of an entire culture, it's better to be politically *incorrect* than to send mixed signals to the people, especially to unaware leaders. That's what got slave descendants in this fix in the first place. Trying to be delicate and tiptoeing around leaders who need help, instead of telling them the plain truth, only creates more confusion. When political dialogue is used while trying to help unaware leaders, they always wind up worse off than they were before help arrived. Trying to be politically correct and resorting to double-talk are gatekeeper tactics and seemingly the only language some intellectuals speak.

Those who take credit for leading the slave culture must awaken. There is still time for them to render a vital service to their people. They are already in the right position and their help is desperately needed. Assisting their people won't get them in trouble with superiors and it won't interfere with their personal finances. *American Slaves, Inc. Renaissance Plan, The Next Step Forward,* will only enhance their lives and elevate their standing in the community. Exposing gatekeepers and gatekeeper positions is a step someone had to take if slaves are to make it all the way to freedom. Telling the unvarnished truth is a commercial tactic that average slaves aren't familiar with. When ASI deals with reality, openly, it is not a political ploy as some might suspect — it is simply good business practice. When seeking financial freedom in the commercial arena, keep in mind that records are kept. Participants must be factual: Descendants of American Slaves are not "African Americans!"

White folks to the rescue

The Uncle Tom syndrome is so utterly damaging to the slave culture that it's important we take a closer look at this mind-set so we can understand how the gatekeeper mentality is transferred from generation to generation by word of mouth and is often disguised as friendship or even leadership. Unaware slave descendants are exposed to this mind-set when they listen to known gatekeepers berate slaves who struggle trying to make slave descendants' situation better. The gatekeeper mentality is extremely poisonous, always has been prevalent but is mostly undetected. Until the books that started the American Slave Movement were published, there was no antidote available because the slavery syndrome hadn't been positively identified and properly exposed.

Uncle Toms try to hide it but it's obvious that slave descendants, at all levels, act a little differently than whites. It's because slaves were bred to have a different attitude and a dissimilar approach to life than whites. This difference is the slavery syndrome, a carryover from servitude. We are just now learning what to do about it. Once victims are infected with the Uncle Tom pattern, even those who vehemently oppose and despise racial discrimination, they still mimic their Uncle Tom leaders, oftentimes becoming carriers of a weak-minded, subservient attitude themselves. The notion that they are the new and improved version of outdated Uncle Toms never crosses their minds. They just know they are living better and will fight anything they think threatens their new lifestyles or personal advancement in life. It doesn't take them long to become alienated from their own people, blind to their surroundings and finally forget from whence they came. ❖

5

I'm Not Angry; I'm Just Doing Business!
(Business mentality acquired)

Testing slave descendants' resolve to do business — *American style*

The time has finally arrived for slave descendants to rise up, leave stagnation behind and begin to move forward. To advance, leaders must drop their false pride, get their heads together and realize they all have something to offer to the American Slave Movement. It's the only way they can take an accurate analysis of slave descendants' collective situation. Once leaders begin collaborating, a starting point can be established and a plan of action that is beneficial to slave descendants and acceptable to commercial America can be devised. It's important that this plan is supported by the religious sector of both the black and white communities. Subsequent to a plan of action being accepted by a cross-section of the population, it could then be introduced as legislation to support a political agenda for the slave culture *(America's Little Black Book,* Page 183, subtitle: "Laying the structural foundation").

Those who lead slave descendants must acknowledge that racial ignorance, the toughest roadblock of all is what has been holding the slave culture back all the time. Acknowledgement is important because racial ignorance is not the same as individual ignorance. Precise steps must be taken to reverse the injected ignorance American Slaves inherited because, even though it started at birth and rose to the top, it now flows from the top down. To move a group of abandoned people forward who are unaware and also have an identity crisis, intelligence must be injected into the *head* of the group *directly*. This sounds difficult but it's not. All leaders have to do is open their minds and accept logic. An admission of ignorance by "African American" leaders will illustrate their ability to accept intelligence. The next step is to initiate a special educational program that encompasses the slave culture simply because slaves were made ignorant because of their pre-planned cultural existence.

Slave descendants must be singled out so America's education system can target their effort toward providing their teachers and other educators with accurate knowledge according to their group's investigated needs, their recorded stagnation and anticipated growth. This step must be headed up by an institution of higher learning and carried out by America's education system in general. The next step is to clarify the legalities of slavery. This is the most imperative step in establishing well-being in the slave culture. If carried out properly, it will ensure that slave descendants are legally recognized as an American people in every area that controls cultural advancement. With this thought in mind, American Slaves, Inc. was incorporated in Kentucky on July 3, 2001. This legal amalgamation marked the official beginning of the American Slave Nation. Government records now show when slave descendants were duly registered with the proper authority, who registered them and why they were registered.

Acquiring startup capital

If we trace the growth of American industry back to the birth of the United States of America, we see that American Slaves were the backbone that helped some of the world's most powerful industrial giants get started. Now these conglomerates are making so much money they either have to pay the bulk of it out in taxes to the government or give it away to charitable organizations. A large percentage of this wealth goes to fund broad-based minority programs. It should be going only to Descendants of American Slaves because they are the only culture that has a legitimate claim to this *overabundance* of wealth — simply because they were instrumental in helping to create it.

True freedom demands that the slave culture be properly remunerated for services American Slaves rendered to the building of America and compensated for their effort accordingly, plus interest. This means ASI, the representing agent, must get this nation's judicial system involved in the American Slave Movement so slave descendants' freedom is legalized, fairly implemented, becomes a part of public record and is then protected. These steps are crucial. They involve laying out the procedure for reparations for slavery through our court system.

Reparations for slavery should be rewarded to Descendants of American Slaves, only, and not to individual "African Americans" who claim they can trace their lineage back *past* slavery to Africa. Reparations for slavery should not be paid to *individual* slaves, period! Slavery wasn't personal or individual — it was business! The business of slavery bred the slave culture; therefore, reparations for slavery should be deposited into a carefully planned slave growth fund that has economic tentacles attached to corporate America. This institution's purpose is to provide avenues for slave descendants to enter the commercial arena. At first, recompense should consist of just enough seed money to get the slave culture up and running. This includes drafting an adequate plan and constructing a sound advancement vehicle.

Overcapitalization could become a huge hindrance if injected too soon. Until a bona fide, long-term plan is drafted and accepted, slave descendants wouldn't know how much money they need, the source of funds, or what to do with *mega* money if they had it. The last thing slave descendants need is an overabundance of capital for unaware leaders to start fighting over and trying to steal. ASI's effort is move the Slave Nation into a position of profitability so they can employ their people. This is the exact opposite of welfare for individuals. When operating at this level, money is simply a tool of the business trade. If slave leaders use resources wisely, their people will prosper. Racial profitability will depend largely on the negotiating skills of their leaders in the field of finance and business. If slave descendants allow "African American" leaders to misuse their collective resources because of racial ignorance, they're out of business before they even get started.

Gatekeeper's worst enemy: the magnifying glass

Slave descendants must start recognizing obvious barriers that stand in the way of their culture merging into mainstream America. These barricades usually go unnoticed, hidden away in plain sight, sucking the very lifeblood out of innocent slaves; except sometimes, they stand out and draw attention to themselves. For instance, the National Association for the Advancement of Colored People stands boldly as a beacon of hope and still clings proudly to the notion that they are a viable institution in slave descendants' fight for freedom, which they clearly are not!

With all the name changes the slave culture has undergone since the NAACP was formed, the very name itself in this day and time sends a confusing signal to everyone, including its own members. Are slave descendants still "colored people" to the NAACP? Is the NAACP simply trying to preserve their historic, but inaccurate name, or have they simply lost touch altogether? Descendants of American Slaves have now reached the stage where they must stop being led by outdated organizations that continually confuse the masses by improperly addressing them. American Slaves must be taught who they truly are.

Some might ask what's in a name. If all of this is so important, why hasn't it been thought of before. Good inquiry. Maybe America at large is submerged in racial ignorance and doesn't fully understand what is transpiring in our great nation. It's quite possible that the American population doesn't know slave descendants were bred in America and what that really means. That's why this author's writings are so important to organizations like the NAACP and to the future of America at large. It is now suspected that racial ignorance in America could be absolute. ASI is pointing out the NAACP because it is the responsibility of companies that supposedly represent slave descendants (Negroes/coloreds/"African Americans") to figure out what the holdup is and why their group lags so far behind other American cultures.

Regardless of where the NAACP stands at the moment on slave descendants' proper identity and lack of progress, it's clear to see that their focus is not on fending for Descendants of American Slaves. ASI met with the NAACP in Louisville, Kentucky, and also in Indianapolis, Indiana. Neither chapter seemed to understand that change is necessary if slave descendants are to rise from the doldrums and begin to move forward.

Regardless of where the NAACP stands at the moment on slave descendants' proper identity and lack of progress, it's clear to see their focus is not on fending for Descendants of American Slaves.

Not understanding America, the NAACP keeps doing little while making public blunders — and then making a big to-do about it. They actually had the nerve to sponsor a mock funeral at their members' expense — to symbolically bury a word! Using a modern day substitution for an offensive expression, they claimed they were putting the "N" word under ground. The funeral was a foolishly contrived media event to keep the NAACP name in the public eye. What did it accomplished? Well, for starters, it exposed the leadership of the NAACP as being self-serving publicity hounds willing to participate in a ludicrous farce hoping the buffoonery would get them a TV sound bite. Apparently fresh out of serious concerns, they launched a circus and made those of us they purport to represent look like clowns. It's not prudent to follow people who are that dense and immature.

Then, on Thursday, June 18, 2009, the NAACP applauded the United States Senate for its passage of a historic resolution apologizing for the enslavement and racial segregation of "African Americans." The article read: "An apology for centuries of brutal dehumanization and injustices cannot erase the past, but confession of the wrongs committed and a formal apology to "African Americans" will help bind the wounds of the nation that are rooted in slavery and can speed racial healing and reconciliation and help the people of the United States understand the past and honor the history of all people of the United States." Then it goes on to state the resolution.

It is hard to express ASI's disappointment with the NAACP. A mere apology for centuries of brutal dehumanization and injustices, written or not, cannot erase the past any more than a mock burial will rid the world of "the N word." How in the world could a confession of the wrongs committed in America, *by Americans,* and a formal apology to "African Americans," who, according to The United States Immigration Service, are foreigners and immigrants, help bind the wounds of the Slave Nation? American Slaves were abused for centuries! The United States Senate can apologize to "African Americans" until "hell" freezes over; it still won't speed racial healing and reconciliation for American Slaves, or their descendants!

It is not the intention of ASI to offend anyone, especially an organization that *once* had a noble mission. It is the job of ASI, however, to tell the people the truth about an outdated organization without hesitation. Slave descendants have been misled far too long already: It's time for the NAACP to regroup, grow up or shut up. Their wasted non-thinking effort is retarding their followers.

Recognizing individual gatekeepers by sight is a difficult undertaking because they themselves may not know they are of the Uncle Tom variety. Recognizing some *institutions* as gatekeeper havens is even more difficult. Some institutions, like the NAACP for instance, have been around for what seems like forever. Slave descendants are so accustomed to viewing these companies as pillars of hope and as an avenue of receiving justice and help that unaware slaves don't recognize them as gatekeeping institutions. These firms didn't start out to be stumbling blocks. America changed and they didn't, and they just wound up out of touch and ineffective. In a changing world, institutions that represent groups of people must learn to keep up with the times because, if they don't, the people they represent get left behind.

The NAACP was around when Dr. King told "Negroes" to head for the "economic battlefield" but they never made a move in that direction. Why not? Because the slave culture is divided and the leadership of the NAACP probably never got the message and even if they did, it's plainly obvious they had little to no idea what Dr. King was talking about.

There are many gatekeeper institutions in America. Be aware: The United Negro College Fund, the National Council of Negro Women, the National Political Congress of Black Women, the NAACP, the Urban League, the Rainbow Coalition, The National Black Chamber of Commerce, NCOBRA, The Congressional Black Caucus and there are *numerous* others — including "African American" churches — all have their constituencies and they purportedly all serve real purposes. Yet, none of them specifically address the Descendants of American Slaves by their accurately identifying name nor do they attend to slave descendants' affairs and special growing needs, and because they don't, they deceive an innocent people. This alone qualifies them as gatekeeper institutions.

As long as American Slaves believe these institutions are representing their culture, they will stay stuck in an unyielding, unconsciousness rut. These companies don't represent Descendants of American Slaves. These businesses are blocking the doorway and keeping slave descendants from being successful. ASI is obligated to bring these powerful institutions together so slave descendants can eventually speak with one voice. It's the only way the slave culture will ever receive justice. Hopefully our words, which might be blunt to some but we consider being true, doesn't offend and alienate leaders who run these high-powered splinter groups. Keep in mind, American Slaves, colored people, "Negroes," "African Americans" and whatever else slaves have been called are at the edge of the "economic battlefield" together and win lose or draw — whether we like it or not — we're all on the same team! If the slave culture fails, America fails. If slave descendants are to excel, these long-established groups that often work at cross-purposes must start working together *in honor of American Slaves!* There is no other way, and no nicer way to say it!

Identifying the guilty

According to fair play, decency and human justice, and because slavery is the cornerstone of American business, Descendants of American Slaves have a legal claim to America's commercial and other business holdings. The debt accrued from slavery is outstanding, the clock is ticking and interest is still accruing. The problem here is, the paper trail of slavery was destroyed and memories faded. Now it's difficult to pinpoint those who were directly involved in slavery. But that's not the end of the story. There can be no statue of limitation on human bondage. The aftereffects of slavery continue. The results of malicious servitude are evident and instantly recognizable. There is evidence of mind manipulation everywhere. Whether the Kentucky Department of Education knew it or not, they measured the aftereffect of slavery on American Slaves when they did the 2008 Kentucky Performance Report on "African American" school children. It doesn't matter that the children were improperly identified; they are still the future of the slave culture.

According to unemployment statistics done by the United States Department of Labor, the long-term aftereffect of slavery on slave descendants who are adults has always been prevalent *and has been measured* but, like the 2008 Kentucky Performance Report, it hasn't been narrated in truthful terms yet. Those assembling the statistics keep misidentifying those who need help by omitting the words American Slave.

So, now what do we do? It's really quite simple. We are Americans and we pride ourselves on doing the right thing. Since slaves were never compensated for decades of forced, dehumanizing labor, ASI says pay the people their due! Some will ask how this can be done. Who could be held accountable for slavery after all this time? Americans also pride ourselves on being able to think, too. Since companies that prospered because of slavery can't be pointed out, ASI figured out the fairest and easiest way to make slavery a win/win proposition for all concerned. We simply refer to "American Slaves, Inc. Renaissance Plan," "The Next Step

Forward, Page 56:

> *"Not all companies in America had a hand in slavery but, because slavery is the cornerstone of American commerce, all companies that are located in America are sitting on the foundation that American Slaves helped build and are functioning within the confines of a nation that was built off the strength of slavery!"*

This tells us that the American Slave culture has the right to file a civil lawsuit against both corporate America and America at large. If the case is argued properly, a sizeable settlement should be forthcoming and would be used as startup capital for the slave culture. Slave descendants have a winnable case if they can accomplish the next two steps. Number one: come up with a plan how to get paid without it destabilizing the American economy or weakening America socially. Number two: get the case into the courts and heard by a jury made up of peers.

ASI is taking serious steps in the right direction but, because of the declining condition of American Slaves' mentality, slave leaders won't participate and, as a result, the pace we are setting is much too slow. Whites are helping but they can't force American Slaves to be free, and they are quick to tell ASI those very words.

Time is actually running out for the slave culture to even get into the commercial race. It takes far too long for slave descendants to carry out simple assignments. For instance, the American Slaves, Inc. Identity Forum should have been a fairly simple chore. Yet, getting the University of Louisville to allow ASI to use their campus as a platform to announce publicly that slave descendants are not "African Americans," but Descendants of Slaves, took better than *two* years! It shouldn't have taken near that long just to announce slave descendants' proper identity. The entire world already knows that America bred slaves. All ASI wanted to do was repeat to the world what the world should already know. The Supreme Court handed down a verdict long ago that declared the exis-

GATEKEEPERS OF THE AMERICAN DREAM

tence of American Slaves and explained how slaves could be properly identified.

In 1839, a mutiny took place aboard the slave ship "Amistad." The takeover was entered into record as being a slave mutiny, which was not true. The black prisoners on board were not slaves. They were natives of Africa who had been captured, bound and then abducted. Ultimately, using intense indoctrination procedure, they were to be processed into slavery by receiving information that would reduce their thinking capability to that of a child. This was done by falsifying information and brutalizing them until they acted a certain way and responded to specific commands. The intent was to reduce the captives in rank from humanoid to beast, or to the level of dumb animals. In the end, they were to be sold as slaves. What made this business venture different from other business deals that involved the capture, transportation and sale of slaves is that during the mutiny, whites were killed — *clearly a no-no!* This was in direct opposition to slaves' indoctrination. Slaves were programmed to *never* harm whites under *any* circumstances! The penalty was death!

A fierce legal battle followed to establish the true identity of the prisoners. If it were established that they were slaves, they would be hanged for breaking the cardinal rule and harming whites. If they weren't born into slavery in America, or hadn't undergone mental rebirth on American soil, they would still be Africans and would be set free and compensated for their trouble and mistreatment. Although the case was won at the federal district court level, it was appealed by President Martin Van Buren to the Supreme Court. Former United States President John Quincy Adams took part in the proceedings. It was during these proceedings that American Slaves' proper identity was legally established and became a part of public record. The outcome of the hearing was clear: Africans are not American Slaves; therefore, Descendants of American Slaves are not "African Americans." Consequently, the captured Africans were set free and returned to their homeland.

America not only *owes* American Slaves, America also *owns* the slave culture and, until documentation declares otherwise, can do whatsoever she desires to slave descendants. All ASI is doing is bringing slave descendants' proper identity to America's attention by pointing out what The United States Supreme Court, established 170 years ago!

The slowdown getting slave descendants' proper identity established at the university level wasn't because the University of Louisville said no; it was because some of those frightened "African Americans" leaders who were guarding the gate of opportunity and acting important didn't realize they are still slaves and therefore didn't know they are hardcore gatekeepers. Like the Uncle Toms of old, they didn't mean any harm; they were just carrying out the master's orders verbatim; not *even* thinking about how much damage was being heaped upon other slave descendants because of those orders. Educators actually thought they were doing a "bang-up" job and, unfortunately, ASI couldn't tell them any better, or there would have been no identity forum.

> *America not only owes American Slaves, America also owns the slave culture and, until documentation declares otherwise, can do whatsoever she desires to slave descendants.*

When the "American Slaves, Inc. Identity Forum" was over, ASI did a simple analysis of the proceedings and shared the findings with top executives. Those contacted cautioned ASI not to publish the results of the debriefing with anyone outside of the organization and some within the organization; thinking exposure would do more harm than good. They warned that openness would surely anger associates in key positions and they would go undercover and retaliate.

They suggested that the analysis should be toned down and be more nonspecific. In other words, they were recommending that ASI replace the hard-truth with a lot of verbiage that held no meaning but would make those who have no idea that they screwed up the event feel good about their poor performances. That way, inadequate leaders could keep right on thinking they did a bang-up job, which is not right because ASI wouldn't have done its job. We would have failed to share important information that could strengthen weak leaders by enlightening them of their failures. Even worse, the leadership of ASI would have failed to strengthen the movement and would have contributed to racial stagnation. This is how frightened gatekeepers make self-motivated people become useless gatekeepers themselves.

At that time, ASI agreed not to expose gatekeepers. We must now look back and ask ourselves if concealing important advancement information was the right thing to do. That's exactly what slave masters did to American Slaves that left the slave culture in this dreadful condition. If slave descendants are to move forward, ASI believes all avenues that lead to freedom must be considered, explored and, if feasible, utilized. Concealing the truth of what we see from our vantage-point could be a terribly wrong move. If the leadership at ASI's is afraid to tell collaborating leaders the absolute truth, this could only mean that collaborating leaders probably won't tell ASI the truth, either, and we're right back to square one. Except this time ASI, like the NAACP, becomes the weakness and failure in the slave culture. ASI leaders afraid to speak the truth is fear-provoking. It's dangerous and, because there is no other entity in America dedicated to uplifting American Slaves, fear could actually lead to cultural demise.

Concealing the truth about those who are not living up to their inherited obligations to their culture stops those involved in the American Slave Movement from knowing what they are doing wrong. If they are never told what they are doing wrong so they can make changes, they will never better themselves so they can rise to a position of accountability. That's why this information on how to recognize gatekeepers is far too important to the advancement of the slave culture to be just skimmed over, read lightly and then hushed up.

Every move ASI has made thus far is predicated on American Slaves having their day and say in an American court of law. It's the only way slave descendants will ever be able to reap any tangible benefits from slavery, and they can't move forward without those benefits! What else would they use for seed money and start-up collateral to get into the economic race? America used the proceeds from slavery and slave labor for startup collateral to help build America. Now that America is successfully built and *hugely* profitable, it's time for America to step up to the plate and fund the American Slave Movement as payback. We're just calling in a long-term debt that is clearly owed and long overdue.

Losing the fight for true freedom is not an option

As ASI prepares slave descendants' court case, winning could very well come down to the mere fact that the slave culture is simply unaware of their plight, which is the awful truth. Attorneys for slave descendants might have to argue that, in their present mental state, slave descendants are incapable of competing in America's economic arena unless their mental handicap is properly addressed and removed. Commonsense tells us that it's impossible for a group of people to compete in America's fast paced, merciless economy if they don't even have the capacity to understand who they are as opposed to those they are competing against.

The downside of pleading ignorance is that highly educated "African Americans" might attempt to repudiate that assertion. They're the ones who started that "African American" lie! Now, having been proven wrong that they are not "African Americans," they might fear a confession of ignorance could jeopardize their *intellectual* livelihoods. Trepidation could cause them to exemplify an even higher degree of ignorance than ASI thought possible. They could still argue that slave descendants don't really exist; that with the passing of time, American Slaves evolved into "African Americans." They might even disagree with the way the United States Immigration Service classifies immigrants. In their state of mind, they could even say the Supreme Court made the wrong ruling.

A normal reaction for many "African Americans" who work in good paying jobs is, from their perspective, things are just fine and dandy the way they are — *at least for them.* Most "high-fliers" are ashamed of their proper identity, frightened about job security and, fearing if they were to take a stand and publicly agree with ASI, it could make waves in the workplace. To keep things quiet and moving along calmly without change, they are willing to settle for less than what they deserve for themselves and seek little to nothing at all for their people. They fail to realize if they were to confess their ignorance by alerting the world they had acquired knowledge, they would be glorified — not damned! When gate-keepers downplay slavery by covering up innovative information that is gathered by grassroots slaves, they are not only blocking their people from advancing, they are stopping their white coun-terparts who could help their situation from receiving accurate information on how to help.

The bulk of gatekeepers moved to the high-rent district a mite too quickly. Now, in addition to being uninformed, improperly identi-fied and made to function under an alias, they are burdened down with too much debt and made to carry around unwarranted racial shame. Whether they know it or not being surrounded by whites in the workplace and sticking out like a sore thumb adds mental pres-sure to a life that is already weighed down with racial embarrassment. Slave descendants with good-paying jobs don't really have a reason to be frightened about job security — if they do their jobs right. Still they are frightened, for good reason, too: *They are not doing their jobs correctly!*

Living up to their inherited responsibility to their culture should be their *main* focus. Far too many slaves suffered and died for the lucky few to forget their people just as soon as they get a good job. Ethnic respon-sibility was here long before they got the good-paying jobs that turned some of them into Uncle Toms. Gaining quality employment went straight to their heads and mingling with upper crust whites made them ashamed of their true identity.

If they understood American business at all, they would realize that when they deny their slave heritage by impersonating Africans, they are denying themselves! There is no shame in being Descendants of American Slaves. If there is shame to be borne because of slavery and because they are slave descendants, it should be borne by whites because they abandoned American Slaves, and by slaves who impersonate "African Americans" because they are ashamed of their true culture. There is no value at all in slaves impersonating "African Americans," only continued squalor.

Retracing our steps through the American Slaves, Inc. Identity Forum

ASI started working with highly educated slave descendants right after we contacted Mr. Robert Byrd who, at the time, was the manager of Jay's Restaurant in West End Louisville. The president of ASI knew Mr. Frank Foster, the builder of the restaurant and wanted to talk to him about teaming with ASI and starting a radio broadcast program from that location and eventually hosting a TV show from there also. We were turning out attention to radio and TV so we could get the word out and let the public know American Slaves had been accurately identified and slavery could now be properly rectified.

We chose that location because it's a beautiful place and the "African American" museum, what some consider a sizeable construction project, is being constructed right across the street. We wanted to keep an eye on some of the money Kentucky is still wasting on "African American" nonsense. We expound on the museum project because slave descendants need to understand that a huge part of the American dream is about America sharing its wealth among the diverse cultures that helped create the wealth. This is done by sharing the proceeds from big money projects among the inhabitants who live in the area where the project is being done.

Our government usually funds nickel and dime projects for "African Americans" as a way of sharing America's wealth with the slave culture. The problem here is, American Slaves aren't mentioned in the language and consequently aren't identified as recipients and therefore don't receive any of the wealth.

The "African American" museum is clearly a misdirection of funds that might otherwise be available to elevate Descendants of American Slaves so they can share the American dream. Unfortunately, because, slave descendants have no idea what is going on, they will never reap any benefits from projects that impact cultures financially. Slave leaders don't have a clue what percentage of big money project American Slaves are due and, if they did, they wouldn't know how to collect. The "African American" museum is nothing more than a *nickel and dime* project donated to weak leaders to pacify their ignorance and keep slave descendants out of the 'mix' and locked out of mainstream America. The last thing American Slaves need is an "African American" museum filled with slave trinkets, African artifacts and glorified junk that's overvalued.

Throwing a few "hungry dogs" a used-up bone to fight over is nothing more than a diversionary tactic that whites have used on slaves from the very beginning of America. The sad part: Even though the African American" museum at 18th Street & Muhammad Ali Boulevard in Louisville, Kentucky, is a nickel and dime project, if the money wasted on that venture *thus far* were in the hands of someone who understand the "economic battlefield," it could have helped free the Slave Nation instead of enriching just a few confused "African Americans!" It's not about how much money you've got. It's about having a leader in charge who knows how to use money to draft a plan that will leverage his followers.

The Ohio River Bridges Project of Kentucky and Indiana is another prime example. This is a project to build and upgrade cross-river facilities in the Louisville, Kentucky area. It too must be shared among residing cultures. It's *already* understood that slave descendants' share of the funds, which would aide in uplifting the slave culture, will be diverted to "African Americans" through "Minority Programs" and then distributed to foreigners. If "African American" leaders start whining about minorities not getting their fair share, they will be thrown another 'bone' to fight over. This tactic keeps "African American" leaders busy scuffling with each other over nothing so the real projects can go forward.

On with the American Slaves, Inc. Identity Forum

At the initial meeting to discuss a radio broadcast, Mr. Byrd was presented with a copy of "America's Little Black Book." He said he would read it and get back to ASI, which he did. At the next meeting, wearing a broad smile and a twinkle in his eyes, he greeted ASI and said he understood the book and that it was long overdue. He stated that it was the first book he had ever read about slavery that didn't upset or anger him. In fact, he said quite the contrary: The book was filled with hope and was very uplifting. Then he told ASI he needed another copy. It seemed his wife had fallen in love with the one ASI had given him and had confiscated it for her own.

ASI accepted Mr. Robert Byrd as a friend, elder and mentor. He started giving the corporation direction and helped assemble the awakening phase of the "American Slave Movement." Unfortunately, before Mr. Byrd could assist ASI further, he passed away. Even though he only gave ASI direction for a very short while, he is thoroughly missed.

It was later learned that Dr. Louise Byrd, his grieving wife, was the Education Gap Coordinator for the State of Kentucky. This meant she already had knowledge of the education gap that existed between blacks and whites. Taking into account that ASI's overall mission is to teach the slave culture how to work together, including acquainting higher educated slaves with their part in the American Slave Movement according to what they do in their daily occupations, Dr. Louise Byrd was in a position of instrumentality to help ASI be introduced to the staff and faculty at the University of Louisville.

Not so fast, there's a gatekeeper in the house!

ASI made its initial alliance with the University of Louisville by funding the "Black High School Educational Summit" and the concurrent "American Slaves, Inc. Identity Forum." The stipulations, however, were agonizing: ASI wasn't allowed to advertise the word slave, American Slaves or Descendants of American Slaves as being the focal point of the summit. After some wrangling over details and fear that black educators would bolt and run for cover and not allow the summit to take place at all, it was finally agreed that we could display a picture of *America's Little Black Book* on the flier with no explanation of why it was there and leave it to the public's imagination to figure out what the summit was all about.

The purpose for not using the word slave on the advertisement is if there was any backlash, the "African Americans" involved in the summit wouldn't be pointed out and identified as trouble making slaves. It's regrettable that we couldn't tell the public what was really taking place at the University of Louisville campus right up front. We wound up hoping the reader could see through the fine print and understand what the campus event was all about. It wasn't whites who made ASI take a back seat to our own show; because of inherited fear and shame, it was educated slave descendants thinking they were "African Americans" who made that decision. They were ashamed of their birthright and afraid to take the lead and make sure slavery was the focus of the summit. They didn't want anyone else to seize the opportunity and spread the news, either, if it meant drawing undue attention to them as being participants in a slave program. At no time during negotiation to hold that summit did whites in any of the meetings object to ASI properly identifying Descendants of American Slaves.

When the topic of financing the summit came up, ASI was cautioned by black educators that the University of Louisville wouldn't shell out one thin dime to make *their educational* summit happen. Whites, however, suggested that money was available to pay for the summit that all we needed to do was talk to the Vice Provost for Diversity and Equal Opportunity. Hearing this, black educators became apprehensive and would have no part of pressuring neither the University of Louisville nor the Kentucky Board of Education for funds that could be used to help slaves.

To get around the *shame glitch* and put their fears to rest, ASI petitioned Louisville politicians for help. Not a chance. When black politicians heard slave descendants were involved, they wouldn't even return our calls. To fund the summit, ASI finally had to go to the only source we knew, a small business that was put in place specifically to help Descendants of American Slaves advance (read: *Black Name, White Game*).

Leading up to the summit, spirits were high and activity was vibrant, but ASI wasn't fooled. From experience we knew our optimism was probably going to be short-lived and problems would surely surface. What bothered ASI the most was that the Minority Teacher Recruitment Project and other educators on the team chose all the speakers for the panel; basing their choices on each prospect's visibility in the community and their ability to arouse a young crowd. Visibility and arousal are important during a presentation and play a huge part in any awakening, but ASI was more concerned with the content of the messages speakers would be delivering to the children than their individual performances and emotional styles.

American Slaves, Inc. chooses the ultimate mouthpiece

It's the duty of elder slaves to put a stop to loudmouth show-offs putting garbage into our children's minds just because someone thinks the words sound cute and are sometimes vulgar. Slave descendants are inherently an arousing people; it's a part of their nature. How well-known black speakers are and how well they deliver a speech might stimulate young, unknowing youth and might even be talked about for a short while by adults. If their words have meaning that will correct the atrocities of slavery and help advance American Slaves, their oratory perpetu-ate indefinitely. Well thought-out messages that have meaning and gives direction toward freedom will bring about continued change for all slave descendants and help them mature mentally so they move forward naturally.

To make certain everyone was on the same page and would deliver the same message that slave descendants are not "African Americans," a couple of days prior to the summit, ASI paid for an expensive dinner to be held at The University Club at the University of Louisville campus and invited all speakers. To make absolutely sure the politicians, digni-taries and educators chosen to serve on the panel had read and agreed with *America's Little Black Book* and were on the same page and would hopefully stick to the topic of slavery, ASI supplied participants with free copies of the book and made it clear that speakers were to explain to these children *and their parents* that the slave culture is improperly identified and what that truly means. Following is the last paragraph of the speech the president of American Slaves, Inc. delivered at the pre-summit dinner:

> *"The future well-being of our children is far too im-portant for us as leaders to get bogged down in our per-sonal agendas. Therefore, allow me to be blunt: It's no longer about business as usual. American Slaves, Inc. is following President Obama's lead — it's time for a change! Anyone speaking at this summit who has not read America's Little Black Book, or doesn't under-stand the message in the book, could do more harm to the American Slave Movement than they do good. Therefore, I'm asking all presenters, please, let's put our personal agendas on hold and get firmly behind the University of Louisville and American Slaves, Inc. and make sure this all-important summit is successful. Help us do our jobs correctly. Slavery is, and always will be, a*

vital part of American history and, because we're in the process of making history — so is this Black High School Educational Summit. Don't let history record that it was we who stood in the way of our people being properly educated, or that we stood in the way of Descendants of American slaves being properly identified so they can advance into mainstream America. Thank you."

At the dinner, something was amiss. Some of those key blacks who are always bragging about what they are doing in the community and hogging the spotlight were given books, plus they reserved seats for the dinner but they didn't show up. This told ASI they had either changed their minds about participating in the summit or, if they participated, they would come with their own agendas.

Dr. Roger Cleveland, Assistant Professor in the College of Education at Eastern Kentucky University, was at the University Club dinner. He heard the president of ASI say what he was trying to accomplish, what he wanted said and how he wanted it said. The other PhD's and educators on the team had been bragging about what a great speaker he was. Hearing such a glorious buildup, ASI was eager to hear this heavily endorsed, dynamic speaker explain American Slave's identity in doctoral terms. Once it was acknowledged that he understood what was expected of him, he was picked to be the keynote speaker at the opening ceremony.

On opening night of the summit, ASI let the crowd know we were there for business and wasn't ashamed to be representing the slave culture. Our speaker didn't jump up and down and run around "strutting his stuff." He instead stood proudly and announced loudly that he was an American Slave. Then he read his speech, verbatim. Every word was precise, to the point and had meaning.

ASI takes this direct approach because American Slaves must create their own paper trail so their offspring will be able to evaluate their culture's progress according to legal documentation and accuracy.

Consequently, all public speeches that reference slave descendants must be truthful, have meaning, and they must be delivered coherently. To create a deliberate slavery paper trail that will stand the test of time, meetings must be held regularly and legal documents must be logged in an orderly fashion.

It's important that slave descendants know exactly where they started, current status, where they are going, mode of transportation and each step leaders are taking to get them there. If American Slaves are to progress, America must be kept aware of what is going on in the American Slave Movement, and leaders must know who the gatekeepers are that are holding slave descendants back.

On the night in question, it soon became clear that Dr. Cleveland was making the same old, tired, meaningless speech he had made many times before. During his entire homily, he never mentioned *America's Little Black Book* or slavery. He just went on and on about how proud he was to be an "African American" and how thankful he was that the university had allowed him to speak. Once he warmed up, he obviously forgot that ASI had asked speakers to stick to the script that the forum was being held to help the children understand that slave descendants *are not* "African Americans" but instead Descendants of American Slaves. He made it a point to gloat about Africa; bellowing that the last four letters in the word African were "i c a n," or I can. Shame on him! What tripe coming from a supposedly educated man! The guest speaker was preaching a clichéd, a *sermon* discounting the very *essence* of *America's Little Black Book* — the topic of the summit!

The opening ceremony sent a conflicting signal to all in attendance — especially to whites who had read *America's Little Black Book* and had publicly agreed with its content. If black educators hadn't been so ashamed of their own culture, they could have really enlightened those kids and their parents of their proper identity and the benefits of their being slave descendants. As it turned out, some of those children, parents and especially whites, probably left that summit more confused than they were before they attended it and ASI can understand why. The president of American Slaves, Inc. is standing at the podium declaring that they are Descendants of American Slaves and Dr. Cleveland, the keynote speaker, is at the same podium preaching they are "African Americans." We were clearly at cross purposes and ignorance was in full bloom. The children, totally unaware, are taught to believe anything their teachers tell them; that's why they go to school. They probably exonerated the ignorant educator and suspected it was the President of American Slaves, Inc. who was submerged in ignorance. Think about it: They could spend the rest of their lives believing they are "African Americans" simply because a noted educator, a PhD no less, told them *exactly* that in the presence of the President of American Slaves, Inc.

> *It's important that slave descendants know exactly where they started, where they currently are, where they are going, how they are going to get there and each step leaders are taking to get them there.*

The President of ASI, realizing the summit wasn't a debate, also realized it wouldn't have been a good idea to get into a heated confrontation with Dr. Cleveland in front of white educators. They already think slave descendants are on a short-fuse, unstable and volatile. It wouldn't have done any good to straighten him out in front of the children, either. After all, he is a PhD and he had *smoothly* influenced them to stay ignorant by reiterating *over* and *over* again that they were "African Americans." The game is not over, though. The next round is coming up and, while we are waiting for the bell to sound, ASI will explore whether Dr. Cleveland is just ignorant and can't learn, or if his performance was a well-thought-out, malicious maneuver. It could be that he never even took the time to read the book.

Educators are in the perfect position to lead the slave culture in the direction of true freedom, simply because the journey starts with slave descendants' proper identity, which is the first step in the education process! Educators are already holding the reins to slave descendants' future in their hands. It would be easy for them to attract the publicity and attention slave descendants need to illuminate their racial failing. It's shameful that "African Americans" are allowed to stay in their respective leadership positions and not produce any meaningful results. The summit was an eye-opener. It taught ASI that slave descendants must develop a leadership agenda consisting of the three main items that are missing from slave leadership: fresh blood, updated intelligence and plain ol' common sense.

To construct a leadership agenda that is inclusive, it's important that those who lead slave descendants realize their individual failures so they can learn from them and they not wind up becoming racial failures. When the leaders of a depressed people fail to recognize what poor jobs they are doing, individually, they are prone to continue doing substandard work for their culture in the future. That's why ASI did an analysis of the proceedings; so everyone, *including* ASI, would know what we did wrong. As a result of the summit, ASI did receive a proclamation from the Governor of Kentucky with the words American Slaves, Inc. on it in fine print. Considering the cover-up of slavery and the ignorance surrounding the slave culture, the proclamation from the Governor is truly an unparalleled beginning. ASI applauds the Governor of Kentucky for recognizing American Slaves, Inc. as the representing agent for the slave culture. We take our hat off to the University of Louisville for allowing American Slaves, Inc. to hold its identity forum on campus: Thanks to all who have thus far been involved in the movement. ❖

6

Gatekeepers in The "Mess Hall"

(The ingestion of poisoned 'mental food')

Smells like unprocessed chitterlings being cooked in here!

In preparation for the American Slaves, Inc. Identity Forum and to kick off the American Slave Movement, ASI held an "Alley Cleanup" to mark the "Awakening" of the movement. The Alley Cleanup, the Identity Forum and everything else ASI has done and is currently doing is in preparation for slave descendants pleading their case in an American court of law. Every event is held to gather evidence to prove who slave descendants are and highlight their plight. When attorneys for slave descendants step into court, they must be prepared to illustrate what transpired during slavery and since that caused the slave culture to wind up in their present declining state. Then they must portray what steps are being taken to correct the atrocities. To plead slave descendants' case intelligently and prove gross, racial neglect, attorneys will need all the evidence that can gather that exemplifies the abuse that happened to American Slaves in the past, what is presently happening to them and what will happen in the future if things don't change.

Some might ask, since everyone already knows that slavery took place and that America bred slaves openly and legally, why not just file a lawsuit against America, state our case and let the chips fall where they may? White board members didn't think that was the smartest thing to do. They feared, even if everyone does know slavery took place, ASI wasn't quite ready for an all-out courtroom brawl where the decision would be final; reasoning, if a lawsuit was filed against America and the trial wound up in an intense courtroom battle and the white population hadn't read *America's Little Black Book* and *American Slaves, Inc. Renaissance Plan,* we would surely make enemies in high places. Without the information in the books being widely read, clearly understood and a large number of whites agreeing with the method ASI is using to rectify slavery, our effort could wind up being for naught. When slaves go into court, they must have documented evidence to support their claim, plus a plan illustrating how to make reparations happen in a peaceful, accepted manner that is clearly understood.

Unfortunately, the news media has continually assassinated the character of slave descendants. Hate has built-up in the white race for the slave culture and mistrust has developed on both sides of the aisle. ASI's attorney feared, even with supporting evidence, white people might not believe ASI's intentions were noble. Because of bigotry and detestation, some whites wouldn't even try to understand what ASI is attempting to accomplish. It was advised that a Moot Court/Mock Trial would yield far better results; recommending that ASI could even use real defense lawyers, prosecuting attorneys, judges and witnesses. That way, slave descendants could plead their case to a group of authentic personnel who are recognized and officially authorized to hear high profile cases and, whether mock or real, they would hand down a fair judgment. According to *America's Little Black Book,* page, 25, properly presenting slave descendants' case to America at large is going to be a tricky proposition that must be handled delicately:

> *"African American attorneys who are filing (for reparations for slavery) might not be properly prepared to argue American Slaves' case. African American attorneys are taught 'law,' but from their dialogue it's obvious they don't understand 'ethnicity.' If African American, or even white, attorneys desire to properly represent slave descendants, they must learn ev-*

*ery aspect of slaves, slavery, and their racial group being born
to America. If any attorney, no matter the nationality, were
to step into a courtroom to represent slave descendants and
not know all about what went into the making of slavery and
their being slaves, they could be walking into a well-baited
trap. Lawyers for reparations are going to have to present their
case to the most brilliant, white minds in America, including
some of America's brightest Uncle Toms — because that's who
they'll be up against."*

Preparing to do battle

In preparation for slave descendants' day in court, we are going to need
astute leadership from those slave attorneys who fully understand
the law or at least who are involved in legal activities and procedure.
Even though they haven't yet realized who they are and, for that reason,
haven't figured out the legalities of slavery, they still inherited the responsibility of leading the slave culture through the legal phase of ASI's
effort to move the slave culture into mainstream America.

Since the Education Summit was over and viewed as a success, especially by those who never fully understood what ASI was trying to
accomplish, the next step on the agenda in slave descendants' advancement was acquiring leadership to head up the Moot Court/Mock Trial.
To start preparing our case, we turned our attention toward the nearest
legal department at the university level. It was suggested that ASI should
contact Mr. Daniel Hall, the Vice President for Community Engagement
at the University of Louisville. He has his Jurist Doctor (Doctor of Law)
degree and, following Dr. Ramsey, is considered to be the second most
powerful person on campus — he turned out to be a Descendant of
American Slaves, aka "African American."

After presenting the vice president with "America's Little Black Book,"
brochures and copies of other books that helped start the American Slave
Movement, he was given a copy of the *American Slaves, Inc. Renaissance
Plan, The Next Step Forward*, to review. To demonstrate that every gate-

keeper knows who the other gatekeepers are who hold slave descendants' future in their hands, ASI was referred to Dr. Blain Hudson, Kentucky's head gatekeeper in Kentucky's "African American" section of the education department. This particular name popping up again was disheartening but, knowing the drill, we just smiled politely, acted political and took it in stride.

The meeting with the Vice President for Community Engagement ended up just like most meetings that involve slave descendants: He evidently didn't think we were serious. He shifted the subject of the meeting from slavery and proceeded to do his demographic "dog and pony show," showing ASI members different graphs that illustrated that the West End of Louisville is a depressed area. It was discouraging to learn that, after all these years, slave descendants who call themselves leaders have come no farther from slavery than doing studies and constructing graphs that illustrate slaves are lost, confused and following dense leaders. Everyone already knows that American Slaves are in bad shape and are pulling up the rear, well behind other American cultures. What they need to know is what their leaders are going to do about it.

ASI was there to find out how to prepare for a Mock Trial in an upbeat manner. After viewing the graphs and knowing they were evidence that could be used during the trial, we now wanted a clearer understanding of whose job it is to correct the atrocities in black neighborhoods and what measures are being taking to put and end to the evils running rampant in inner cities. ASI understands that it's probably not even the University of Louisville's job to correct racial ills but they did they study and he's the one who pulled out the graphs and quoted the statistics. Once he put information on the table that had something to do with American Slaves, ASI automatically started searching for answers. Realizing that we're all in this bind together and people at the university level are supposed to be the most intelligent among us, ASI figures that universities should be held responsible for coming up with solutions.

The rectification of slavery will no doubt end up in a fierce courtroom battle. ASI was hoping an institution of higher learning, even if they say it's not their job to correct racial ills, could direct our efforts as we fend for slave descendants in the legal arena. Unfortunately, the Vice President for Community Engagement has since become unreachable, and ASI understands why. If the best that "African American" leaders in the field of education can do is tell American Slaves, Inc. that something is wrong in the slave culture and spend their time drawing graphs that illustrate the obvious, they're worthless and it's best they are unreachable.

The meeting was not a complete bust, though: ASI learned another important feature of gate-keeping: It's called 'exclusion,' which is inaccessibility, the most commonly used gatekeeper tactic. That's why the American mainstream has always been inaccessible to slaves. When their leaders rise up, they become unreachable but you must pay close attention or you won't recognize the *inaccessible* transformation.

Everyone already knows that American slaves are in bad shape and are pulling up the rear, well behind other American cultures. What they need to know is what their leaders are going to do about it.

Even though ASI and the Vice President for Community Engagement agreed to meet again after he had a chance to examine the documents, ASI finally gave up trying to maintain contact. After calling numerous times and waiting the required time between phone calls and no return calls or emails, ASI members had no other choice but to conclude that the Vice President had declined our offer to lead ASI's effort in the "Moot Court/Mock Trial" phase of the American Slave Movement, or doing anything else to help his people, and was using inaccessibility to make sure ASI got the message.

The Vice President for Community Engagement becoming unreachable put ASI in a precarious situation. What were we to do now? Before trying to move forward, we had to figure out what we were doing wrong. With crime on the rise and the killings in the West End of Louisville escalating and knowing this and other negative condition exist nationwide, ASI couldn't just halt the movement, stop doing our jobs and alter our advancement schedule simply because an "African American" leader was using an age-old gatekeeper tactic by keeping his head down and refusing to take ASI's calls. Slaves don't have options; so what can slaves do in cases like this? One thing for sure, before trying to move forward, we had to figure out what we were doing wrong — if in fact we were doing anything wrong.

Instead of ASI allowing an eluding tactic to halt forward movement, we got busy figuring out a better way of moving on; keeping in mind that it's best to be careful when trying to maneuver around high-powered gatekeepers. They not only belong to a network that is tightly run; they have a firm grip on slave descendants' future and have been known to be vicious and downright sneaky when they think their cover has been blown.

As frustration set in, ASI decided it was time to go straight to the top before stagnation took over. So we went over the vice president's head and scheduled a meeting with Dr. James Ramsey, president of the University of Louisville. After conferring with board members and meeting with other advisors, however, it was brought to our attention that, even though the Vice President for Community Engagement obviously didn't want to be involved in the movement and was intentionally ignoring us, he would still be highly offended if we went over his head to his boss. He was in a position to block ASI's further advancement at the university; thus keeping a choke-hold on slave descendant students. If we were to anger him, he could go down in history as being the Uncle Tom who stopped slave children from being properly educated without even knowing it. ASI was in a very unstable situation: We were dealing with a person who had the power and was in the right position to push ASI back to square one.

To hopefully avoid gatekeeper wrath, it was decided it would be a better idea to let others in the Community Engagement department know what we were doing. There might be someone in the department who would want to know what ASI was doing and might even want to become involved. We therefore approached the vice president's assistant, Dr. Ralph Fitzpatrick, and a meeting was scheduled for July 23, 2009. At the meeting, we brought the vice president's assistant up to speed on the "American Slave Movement." We also informed him of what went on at the meeting we had with his boss, the Vice President for Community Engagement. We then alerted him of the upcoming meeting we had already scheduled with Dr. James Ramsey. We let him know *up front* that all meetings that involve Descendants of American Slaves are documented and records are kept and are available to the public.

The paperwork we gave the assistant was an overview of slave descendants' abandonment since slavery. It highlighted what had taken place in the movement and showed that ASI had reached the point where we needed guidance and support from President Ramsey and his staff.

Gatekeepers in the snack bar

Having already met with Mr. Larry Cox, aide to U.S. Sen. Mitch McConnell of Kentucky, prior to meeting with the Community Engagement Department at the University of Louisville, ASI went over the Kentucky Performance Report 2008 with Dr. Fitzpatrick and shared what Mr. Cox had told us: that ASI should try to utilize the McConnell Center at the University of Louisville to better understand how leadership really works. When Community Engagement heard this, it was suggested that ASI instead use Porter Scholars at the University of Louisville to start a leadership discipline targeted at slave descendants similar to that at the McConnell center. This was good news. It showed that Community Engagement might be interested in slave descendants' fate after all. If they really were concerned and such a connection could be made, it would be the first time that a noted University teamed with slave leaders to openly teach slave descendants how to be effective leaders for their people using their accurately identifying racial name.

It was comforting hearing the vice president of the Community Engagement Department suggest the same approach that Mr. Larry Cox had suggested, except he was suggesting using a different group. This suggested a diversion and it sent up a red flag because Porter Scholars is a predominantly black program named in honor of an "African American" who, in reality, is a slave descendant. ASI wonders if the University of Louisville realizes there is a difference! Keep in mind, ASI's ultimate mission is to fight ignorance wherever we find it! The McConnell Center is a facility named in honor of U.S. Senator, Mitch McConnell, a white *sitting* Senator. Was ASI being asked, or being told, to choose sides in what appeared to be a racial competition where slave descendants would surely come out on the losing end? That's what ASI is fighting against. We are not trying to keep whites and blacks at odds. We're trying to bring about cohesiveness that will benefit the slave culture.

ASI cheerfully agreed to contact Porter Scholars. What else could we do? After all, we asked the man for direction and he was directing us. But now we were wondering if we should follow his directions. On a daily basis in a hands-on situation, a sitting Senator could surely help slave descendants more than a deceased "African American" could. We're still talking business here. The red flag was raised because there were now two entities on the table and ASI was in essence being asked to make a decision and being told what that decision should be; realizing full well that if the American Slave Movement turns into a "black thing," it won't work!

Thinking ahead, because ASI's attorney was already in the process of preparing for slave descendant's day in court and to make sure whites stayed at the forefront of the movement, ASI told Community Engagement that what we needed right away was a strong, well-worded proclamation from President Ramsey endorsing ASI's upcoming Moot Court/Mock Trial. Community Engagement told us that would be no problem. Hearing this, ASI representatives' spirits were lifted. ASI's Moot Court/Mock Trial would soon be officially endorsed by Louisville's top white educator at the college level, making it a moot point which leadership entity we utilized for leadership courses.

As the meeting was winding down, Community Engagement enlightened ASI to a new aspect of gatekeeping and how it worked at the University of Louisville, sharing that President Ramsey had an African American "kitchen group," explaining that everyone knows there is a racial problem in America but, unfortunately, those in the white culture who have the authority to correct racial ills act as if they don't understand what the problem is in the "African American" community or either they don't want to be bothered with fixing it. For that reason, "African American" leaders from the slave culture are handpicked and put

We are not trying to keep whites and blacks at odds. We're trying to bring about cohesiveness that will benefit the slave culture.

into positions where they can solve their own people's problems. The Community Engagement representative made it a point of bringing to ASI's attention that President Ramsey was different from other white leaders, expounding that he was a good man and was truly interested in the welfare of the West End of Louisville, the epicenter of the slave descendants' culture in Kentucky.

The term *kitchen group* was new to ASI and we asked him to explain the mechanics of how it really worked. The Community Engagement representative told us that a kitchen group's job is to inform white leaders, which in this case would be President Ramsey, of what must be done to achieve whatever goal is sought. ASI's contingent assumed, because the associate vice president was a slave descendant and an educator to boot, the ultimate goal would be closing the education gap that exists between "African Americans" (slave descendants) and white children. This was exciting news. It sounded exactly like what slave descendants need to bridge America's racial gap: a kitchen group for support. American Slaves, Inc. is not a kitchen group, but we serve the same worthwhile purpose to America that U of L's kitchen group serves for President Ramsey. A major ASI function is to supply accurate information to those in positions to rectify the negative aftereffects of slavery and the deteriorating condition of slave descendants.

The red flag flies at half-staff

Hearing that President Ramsey would probably act on what the kitchen group suggested and then follow through on the approach ASI was proposing, all the pieces were finally falling into place. Dr. Fitzpatrick, the associate vice president, would make an excellent leader for slave descendants: He is highly educated and well-versed. When he speaks, people listen; but was he really listening to ASI and taking our effort seriously? Were we all on the same page or was he just being political and saying encouraging words that he says at all meetings that concern slave descendants? Was he mimicking his boss and saying what he thought we wanted to hear so the meeting would soon be over with on a good note?

Sometimes, "African American" leaders, not realizing that ASI is a serious enterprise, thwart our efforts and slow down progress without even realizing it. ASI was already in the process of following the suggestion of Larry Cox, Senator McConnell's aide, to make use of the McConnell center at the University of Louisville to better understand how leadership really works. Community Engagement was sending us in an entirely different direction, telling us to contact "Porter Scholars."

The reason why ASI was second-guessing the U of L Community Engagement department is because, if Community Engagement was truly interested in helping slave descendants, it seems that upon hearing ASI's mission and realizing the dire situation their people are in, they at least would have undertaken the task of contacting the Porter Scholars themselves instead of telling ASI to do it. It's bothersome that slave descendants who are already in position to help their people and are being paid to help act this way. "African American" leaders must muster the gumption to step up to the plate and do their part. It's their duty to carry-out the jobs their foreparents left for them to do instead of pawning people off on someone else.

When we told Dr. Fitzpatrick that a meeting had already been arranged with President Ramsey for July 24, 2009, he asked us to reschedule the meeting so he could be there. Hearing this, the ASI group was confident that everyone was on the same page and optimistic that the kitchen group concept really worked. On August 7, 2009, ASI and Community Engagement met with President Ramsey and gave him in writing what we needed from him and showed him the video ASI had filmed at the American Slaves, Inc. Identity Forum.

President Ramsey was visibly impressed with the video and the written request ASI had carefully prepared. Dr. Ramsey suggested that ASI and Community Engagement should jointly contact U of L's Louis D. Brandeis School of Law which was located on campus and discuss the Moot Court/Mock Trial with them. He then gave us the name of the person ASI and Community Engagement should talk to. ASI was overjoyed, but something was out of focus and didn't set right. ASI has been trying to free slaves for a long time. Getting people to cooperate and do their part is usually like pulling healthy teeth using rusty pliers without anesthesia. It's typically a painful undertaking, but this was *way* too easy. It started us to wondering what would happen next.

Never get your hopes up when dealing with ignorance disguised as intelligence

It was during this experience that ASI found out another reason why whites are nonresponsive and slow to react to the rectification of slavery. Like the Community Engagement staff said: White leaders aren't close to slave descendants' problems. ASI found out however that whites must be totally disconnected from the real problem. Perhaps it started when whites formed advisory kitchen groups for various endeavors. In this particular case, whites made the fatal mistake of selecting the usual "African Americans" to fill these advisory slots but they failed to recognize the *huge* disconnect between the kitchen group membership and the people the group is supposed to serve.

Sweeping change in black communities is *desperately* needed but, unfortunately, it seems impossible to achieve. When whites who have the authority to make change happen are contacted for advice, direction or assistance, they receive the same mixed signals from kitchen groups they have always received from unaware people who don't understand the real situation. The people who make up these groups are already doing well. They don't feel the pain of stagnation and deterioration gnawing away at the very soul of our sick nation. They show no urgency *whatsoever* about the rectification of slavery. Not understanding that it's their people who are suffering, their attitude is the same as uncaring whites: It's just business as usual; everything is fine; just keep things moving along as they are. Gatekeepers have created a bottleneck in the slave culture and there seems to be no way for grassroots slave descendants to go around it without making waves.

Kitchen groups have *no concept* of America's true racial situation. This is evidenced by them not fully understanding slave descendants' worsening condition. When meetings are held to discuss racial issues, they offer the same verbiage they always spout — what they think whites want to hear. Then when the meeting is over, they use the same failed methods and worthless tactics they've always invoked — what they think whites want done. They absolutely refuse to think on behalf of their people!

It's as if slave educators are puppets on a string and nobody's pulling the cord. They think they are elite but, in the full light of day, it is realized they are only introverted parasites feeding off their own pabulum. They aren't in contact with their true culture or connected to their mortal roots and it doesn't seem to bother them one bit. It's as if they are in a fluctuating daze, going from meaningless meetings to futile gatherings — and then the "catch 22" starts all over again. They just lumber along at the same foot-dragging gait they've gotten used to, performing their individual jobs, complaining about how rough the job is and, all the time, getting nothing done. Assimilation has taken its toll and they think they are really doing something important for their people, and they're not.

It is established that there is a wide cultural gap between whites and blacks in America but ASI found out that the real disparity that's destroying Descendants of American Slaves lies within their own culture, not between whites and blacks. Whites have proven they are *more* than willing to help slave descendants. They just need the go-ahead from "African American" leaders. Unfortunately, black leaders are frightened out of their minds of speaking up for their people, which is by no means surprising. It was because of fear that they started impersonating "African Americans." At this stage, they wouldn't dare ask whites for help in the name of slaves. They think it would make them appear frightened and ignorant. They don't seem to realize that refusing to speak up for American Slaves — *their very own people* — proves they are scared! And not realizing their peoples' proper identity removes all doubt that they are ignorant.

When the meeting was over and it was suggested that we hastily follow up on Dr. Ramsey's suggestion to contact U of L's Brandeis School of Law, the kitchen group had a ready excuse why they couldn't mobilize within the time frame President Ramsey suggested. The Associate Vice President of External Affairs announced that Dr. Ramsey already had his department busy raising $10 million for the University and, therefore, he would be spending most of his time in Washington,

> *Whites have proven they are more than willing to help slave descendants. They just need the go-ahead from "African American" leaders. Unfortunately, black leaders are frightened out of their minds of speaking up for their people, which is by no means surprising. It was because of fear that they started impersonating "African Americans."*

DC. ASI wonders why he waited until after the President had left the room to say that. He should have said it when the President first suggested we contact U of L's Brandeis School of Law, or at least before he left the room.

Dr. Fitzpatrick was proud that the University of Louisville had entrusted him with such an important mission and, while ASI was proud of him, too, we were hoping at some point he would remember who he was and the condition of his people. Maybe then he would have understood the urgency of introducing ASI to the University of Louisville Brandeis School Of Law in a timely fashion. If he fully understood his people's situation, he would have been asking whoever he was meeting with that was going to donate *$10,000,000* to the University of Louisville, which is already a flourishing entity, to first donate just a *few* dollars to American Slaves, Inc. to help fund the American Slave Movement.

ASI never did get the well-worded proclamation from President Ramsey endorsing ASI's upcoming Moot Court/Mock Trial. Some uppity gatekeepers, while embellishing their own importance and spouting their well-rehearsed platitudes, go out of their way to insult ASI membership's intelligence by downplaying the need to rectify slavery. The truth of slavery and ways to rectify the mental condition slavery left the slave culture in is too vitally important to be stifled by those who are in position to help remedy situation.

To keep from hurting gatekeepers' feelings by pointing out their inadequacies, it is often suggested that ASI be diplomatic and not tell the blatant truth about what is going on in America. The reasoning is if ASI were to tell the truth and call some well-known gatekeepers out by name, they would try to destroy the movement and not even realize their actions could set slave descendants back many more years. That's how rigid, yet unstable ignorance is in the slave community and how fragile true freedom is for slave descendants. We at ASI believe Descendants of American Slaves really want to be free. They can't reach freedom, however, if their leaders can't direct them toward freedom's door because they have no concept of what true freedom really is. Ordinary slaves don't know the necessary steps to take that would lead them out of bondage.

"African American" leaders are out in front. It's their job to know the way to freedom or get busy learning how to "blaze a trail." They are supposed to listen closely to their constituency and respond to problems in an honest and thoughtful manner. After hearing the cries of their followers, it becomes their responsibility to figure out a plan how to improve racial conditions for their people. It's a leader's calling to be instrumental in implementing whatever plan is drafted in a timely fashion. The problem here is, because of their impeccable credentials, "African American" leaders think they already know it all. They absolutely refuse to follow a plan drawn up by their un-credentialed constituents even though the un-credentialed are closer to the problem than the "know-it-all-credentialed" are. If someone comes up with a plan how to help slave descendants, and the person with the plan is not held in high esteem with kitchen groups, "African American" leaders won't even consider the plan. ASI disagrees with those who say we should be politically correct when dealing with those who may be educated but are otherwise misguided and unaware. Being too political is the very reason why slave descendants are stuck in a ruinous, declining rut. At some point, if we are to turn this thing around and

> *Being too political is the very reason why slave descendants are stuck in a ruinous, declining rut. At some point, if we are to turn this thing around and reverse the negative aftereffects of slavery before it's too late those who lead slave descendants must speak the blatant truth, at least to their own people, without fear of reprisal!*

reverse the negative aftereffects of slavery before it's too late, those who lead slave descendants must speak the blatant truth, at least to their own people, without fear of reprisal!

The real difficulty of helping slaves: Gatekeepers in the pulpit

In order for slave descendants to be the best that they can be, someone must summon up the courage to look their leaders dead in the eye and tell them straight-out just how bad a job they are really doing and why. ASI is attempting to do just that. Unfortunately, thus far we don't have the ear of "African American" ministers and preachers have the ear of the masses. They claim to be leaders but are unresponsive to the needs of their followers. They act as if it blasphemy to work jointly with diverse organizations for a common cause.

It's about time the leaders of the religious community woke up, wised up, stopped sucking blood and got involved. Black ministers should start paying attention to their people's real needs and learn how to lead their followers properly. This means they must understand who they are, whom they are leading, where they are going and when they will reach their destination.

The majority of black preachers are becoming nothing more than parasites feeding off their own peoples' misery. Trying to reason with some of them is next to impossible because they think they already know it all. The saddest part, most preachers are too "set in their ways" to even consider changing. They figure why should they change what is already working *just fine* for them. It's difficult to get black preachers to listen to anyone except themselves; so how in the world could ASI get them listen to a person trying to sell them on the idea of reviving slavery who doesn't attend their church and contribute money to help support their high standard of living? The answer is simple. We're all going in the same direction and no slave can be truly free unless all slaves are mentally free. Freedom must be inclusive! All slaves must advance to freedom together, saint, sinner, rich and poor.

ASI would never ask anyone to do something that any member at ASI wouldn't do. By the same token, ASI would never ask ministers or anyone else to forsake their religious beliefs. The American Slave Movement is not about religion or spiritual beliefs. The ASI movement is about strengthening America. This means speaking the truth and seeking justice. ASI doesn't want to tussle with religious organizations, nor do we wish to compete with ministers preaching the prospects of heaven and "hell" after death. It's not our mission to steal church members! ASI was put in place to help preachers more especially, so they could help their members who are slave descendants rise above obvious degradation so they can make it to freedom while they are still here on earth.

It is not wrong to preach freedom on earth. That's what America is supposed to be all about, anyway. Yet, until Gospel Missionary Church stepped up to the plate and Bishop Dennis V. Lyons, pastor, heeded the call, took the oath and preached *straight* from *America's Little Black Book*, not one church in America had preached about the long-suffering of American Slaves, the continued mental subjugation of slave descendants, nor the condition slavery left the slave culture in.

To know what to do about Descendant of American Slaves' identity crisis and economic shortfall, slave descendants need to hear from the many pulpits in America they in fact have an economic setback and that it's because of their identity crisis. To hear the simple truth that they are Descendants of American Slaves who only thought they were "African Americans" would lift the spirit of the Slave Nation. Slave descendants would finally know what is wrong with their people and why they are viewed in a different, negative light. Just knowing that they are America's first and only born group of people and that ASI already has a plan that will advance the slave culture would make slave descendants' spirit soar. It would be their rallying point.

Churches could be the arrangement that brought American Slaves together. In fact, even though it's a longshot, they could even be responsible for American Slaves choosing one leader so they could speak with one voice! If slave descendants were to build their culture on the foundation of togetherness and use their proper identity as the cornerstone of their being, it would assure that slave descendants' birthright endures perpetually and securely. If the aftereffects of slavery are clearly understood by members of the clergy and if they were to start preaching the truth about slavery, a mental transformation would automatically take place.

Think about it, if churches got involved that would mean masses of people coming together. As a group, they could insist that resources that are currently being wasted on piecemeal programs that largely benefit foreigners and minority groups be utilized properly to help their people. The end result could alleviate Descendants of American Slaves' dire condition and uplift the Slave Nation without it destabilizing our nation's economy. An upgrade of slave descendants' mentality, would create a win/win situation for all Americans. This upgrade would consist of nothing more than preachers doing their job and telling their followers the *basic* truth. The possibilities derived from the true rectification of slavery are astounding for descendants of slaves and also descendants of slave masters.

Churches, you're up! So, preachers, what's your call?

Groundbreaking news should be shouted from the pulpit loud and clear. Such is the news that slavery can now be truly rectified! Hearing from the clergy that true freedom can now be obtained would give slave descendants the hope a dejected people need. Even in a confused, depressed state of mind, ignorant slaves would eventually understand this kind of truth. Churches are supposed to stand firm for what is right and take a solid, unyielding stand against what is wrong. The continued debasement of slave descendants is wrong!

If preachers were to come together and help ASI get slave descendants' case aired in a court of law and heard by a jury made up of peers, this one common cause would change slave descendants' racial condition and the course of their depressing history almost overnight. It would be the first time slave descendants cried out for justice with one intelligent, legible voice with a plan *in hand* how justice could be administered diplomatically. The main reason why slavery hasn't been rectified or dealt with is, until the publication of *America's Little Black Book,* no one understood how to approach talking about slavery or how to make reparations for slavery happen without all "hell" breaking loose.

African American ministers have emerged as America's main gatekeepers. Unfortunately, they're limiting God's supremacy simply because they don't know who they are. If they don't know who they are, they couldn't know who they're leading. If they don't know who they are leading, they couldn't possibly know what kind of intercession to ask of God that would help their followers. It's time for black churches to heed the call and fulfill their intended purpose *in this day and time* — and not merely wait for a "heavenly reward" that in many cases won't be granted because it hasn't been earned.

To advance economically, slave descendants must learn to use *whatever* is at their disposal to move ahead — and this includes the *many* houses of worship located throughout their neighborhoods. Churches are God's way of giving American Slaves an advancement weapon in the form of a communication point. "African Americans" leaders just fail to recognize it. Churches have always been a spiritual shelter where slaves, and now their descendants, have gathered to receive guidance in their everyday lives and hope for a brighter future. Slaves weren't allowed to read and write, know their earthly existence or receive accurate racial information; they did however have this continuous communication system within easy reach. The problem here is churches haven't recognized their mission because they haven't read *America's Little Black Book.* It explains the churches role in advancing American Slaves into mainstream America.

During slavery, churches gave an accurate depiction of those dark-skinned people who were bred in American for one purpose only, to be slaves, but not anymore. Without accurate information concerning slaves and slavery, those who claim to be the leaders of slave descendants can't tell their followers who they are, how far the slave culture has come, or how far they have to go to be *truly* free. To plan slave descendants' future intelligently in regard to their current negative circumstance, leaders must understand what brought the slave culture to its present station, what that station truly is and why stagnation has set in. The average ministers probably wouldn't admit the truth and give an accurate account regarding slave descendants' racial stagnation because it would incriminate them. Preachers omitting slavery from their ministry, because they don't understand the aftereffects of human bondage, is the most prevailing reason why slave descendants are running behind.

Slave descendants need to hear a message from the pulpit that all modern day slaves can relate to. This means preachers need a common denominator. That common denominator is — *and always has been* — slavery! At slave descendants' present stage and condition and in their confused state of mind, they need to receive a straightforward, understandable message that gives specific directions for their entire nation from the only group of leaders the majority of slave descendants will listen to — their preachers! How else can Descendants of American Slaves make decisions that could improve their deteriorating condition in their own homeland? How else will they as a people understand what is happening to them and why they are treated inferior to other cultures that has come into their motherland if their leaders refuse to tell them who they are racially? How can slaves that were abandoned in ignorance know which way to go if their own leaders won't communicate with them, lead, guide and direct them?

There should be one *root source* that all slaves can draw from for their betterment. This source must speak a factual language, without hogwash and political double-talk in a manner that slaves can and will heed. Slave leaders appear to think there is no reason for slave descendants to be together or communicate properly. "African American" churches might have the ear of the masses but unfortunately they are not saying anything that will fortify the slave culture. This makes them more or less useless to the advancement of their people.

ASI takes its share of the blame

Casting some doubt on ASI's accumulated wisdom, could it be that we are not communicating the wisdom we have gathered to other leaders properly? Are we somehow missing the mark? After all, ASI is bringing straight-thinking, no-nonsense innovation on the behalf of slaves to the table; something that wannabe "African Americans" aren't used to. ASI is a business institution run by those who have business mentalities. The people that we are criticizing (hopefully in a constructive manner) are ministers, teachers, politicians and other activists that run splinter groups.

Out of all probability, they aren't accustomed to the business tactics ASI is using or the blunt and, according to some, thoughtless way we speak about our constituents. The leader who incorporated ASI is a seasoned businessman. He suspects, according to the seriousness of the situation, the message should be even stronger.

To most leaders in the slave culture, industry has to be a whole new ball game and the most frightening place on earth, and they're right; it truly is. Slave descendants who think they are "African Americans" must understand that there is no security on the economic battlefield and business doesn't tolerate losers. Because of the lack of proper communication, the slave culture has no concept of how business is really done. Few Uncle Toms have been to the "frontline" of the economic battlefield and engaged in industrialized combat with "no holds barred." Gatekeepers actually think they are doing good business when they spout meaningless political double-talk at meetings that holds no meaning and use snide business tactics on ordinary slaves who are defenseless, or either when they purposely avoid slave leaders who try to help the defenseless. Gatekeeper stupidity has kept the slave culture abandoned and confused.

Back to the pulpit

As a "test project," just so ASI would have an idea if churches in Kentucky would support the American Slave Movement and to make sure they had fresh, updated information in their hands, ASI sent 50 copies of "American Slaves, Inc. Renaissance Plan," "The Next Step Forward," to 50 "African American" churches that belong to the "General Association of Baptists in Kentucky." The cover letter stated that the book was free. We asked each church to send $15 to support the American Slave Movement and help defray the cost of printing and shipping. ASI wanted to know just how many churches would understand the necessity of rectifying slavery and respond. We also wondered what reason any church would have for not responding to such an urgent plea and such a small amount of support.

Only one church out of 50 responded. ASI doesn't know why churches didn't respond. Maybe they couldn't afford the $15, but we have a good idea why St. Stephens, purported to be the largest "African American" church in Kentucky, didn't respond. We elaborate on this because this church is in a leadership position, has a large following and that's what this entire book is all about: leadership and "follow-ship." ASI hopes the pastor of St. Stephens didn't misunderstand the reference made in *America's Little Black Book* to an article that was in the newspaper.

On February 8, 2004, Dr. Kevin Cosby, the minister of St. Stephens, was quoted by *The Courier-Journal,* **Kentucky's leading newspaper,** as saying: *"There's not a need for a commander in chief ...There's a need for commitment to change."* Naturally, ASI disagrees with such an asinine statement. Any knowledgeable leader would also take exception. America is founded on astute leadership. Without a smart commander and chief **there is no commitment to change.** That's why we have a presidential election every four years — *to elect a **commander in chief!*** Hopefully ASI *quoting* what the pastor of this *wealthy* church said didn't stop them from contributing $15 dollars to the American Slave Movement. Because, whether they know it or not, they are a part of the movement and the movement needs and deserves their support.

It's unfortunate that "African American" leaders don't accept constructive criticism very well. Actually, *America's Little Black Book* didn't criticize Dr. Cosby, only. There were a total of five of Louisville's "black leaders" featured on the front page of Louisville's leading newspaper, all commenting on *black leadership* in Kentucky. ASI is not to blame for shedding light on their ignorance. By showing off for the news media, they did it to themselves! The other four, their comments and ASI's rebuttal are as follows: Ricky Jones, University of Louisville professor, States, *"There is no black political leadership in this city."* Cheri Bryant, District 5 Metro Council member, states, *"You still need the tree shakers ... people who are unbought, who can speak freely."* Junior Bridgeman, businessman and chairman of University of Louisville board of trustees, states, *"Young people today ... aren't looking for one person ruling."* The Rev. Louis Coleman, Justice Resource Center director, states, *"If you didn't experience the troubles of the '60s, the blatant segregation, you don't really feel the pain."*

ASI doesn't discriminate. The ASI president's comment was directed at trying to help all of them. He simply wrote:

> *"The above quotes are just a sample of the backward, confused, black leadership in Kentucky; I'm quite sure it's the same all across America. It is obvious our current leadership doesn't have a plan for the future of our people. These people are not our leaders because we haven't chosen them to be so, and it's not right for them to be passing themselves off as such. Once we become a recognized people and have a true leader there is a possibility these people might take their cue from our cabinet of leaders, of which they very well could become a part of. However, this can happen only if they are chosen and are willing to be team players and, most of all, if they are capable of learning.*
>
> *"American Slaves must stop these little groups from claiming us, confusing us, dividing us up and then acting like they don't know why we can't get together. Our leaders are the reason we can't get together, and the main reason we are racially*

confused and always tagging along behind other American groups. Present day special interest groups do not represent the descendants of slaves because they are not leading us as a group. American Slaves must be able to choose our leader from candidates who make pledges to American Slaves. Those elected should only be reelected when promises are kept."

Instead of thanking whoever is trying to help them by telling them their faults and weaknesses and telling them what is *really* going on in America, "African American" leaders shun the only corporation that is willing to tell them the truth. How can ASI tell preachers there is a problem in their group and that *they* are the problem and what to do to help the situation if ASI is not allowed to be truthful with ministers without them retaliating and trying to destroy whatever plan is available? If leaders won't listen to their constituents telling them that they're the problem, what else is left to do except expose them as inadequate and disqualify them from being leaders. As of now, gatekeepers truly have Descendants of American Slaves in a pickle.

When ASI first undertook the chore of providing a road map to rectifying slavery, we went to black leaders and asked them to help start the American Slave Movement. Half wouldn't listen because they were afraid. The others, blinded by greed and enjoying "African American" prosperity, refused to recognize slave descendants' true condition. As far as they are concerned, there is no problem and nothing to rectify.

Many people have said that ASI is "hung up on leadership," and they are right. Then they ask why ASI would be searching for someone to lead the slave nation when ASI already has a leader in the driver's seat who claims to know so much about leadership. It's simple: The Slave Nation must function as America does. Leadership must be changed continually to avoid stagnation. Our leader is constantly seeking other leaders who have or can acquire a clear vision of the future, courage and insightful wisdom. The goal is to replace the Uncle Toms who are in control of slave descendants' destiny. They have been parading as leaders and leading slave descendants down the wrong road far too long already. There has to be a changing of the guard! ASI's current president will be the president of American Slaves, Inc. and lead the American Slave Movement for his prearranged term, only. His orders are explicit: Awaken the American Slave Nation! Get them up, turned around and functioning! He accepted the challenge.

A good leader not only realizes his proper racial identity. He also understands that his time is limited and he must get his job done before his time runs out. It's his duty to understand his people's condition, comparatively and figure out their destiny. President Shelton is continually seeking better leadership, based on need, to take his place while all the time steering his followers toward cultural success. ASI's mission statement is clear: Our goal is to elevate slave descendants. To do that, we must take a different approach than various splinter groups have taken in the past.

Change, the ultimate advancement weapon

To make sure ASI is different and uses an entirely new approach, instead of being ashamed of slavery, our goal is to extract points of pride from slavery and inject those positives into slave descendants. Then we're going to put some dignity into the gatekeeper position. Yes, there is pride in slavery and the gatekeeper position could be a respectable, sought-after station for assertive leaders who are astute and understand that America is a country founded on business and who understands what that means.

ASI wants the best person available to lead the slave culture. Those who understand leadership and think they can do a good job leading the slave nation should let American Slaves, Inc. know. We will see to it that their name gets on the ballot. If they can illustrate they can do a better job and can produce a written plan to that effect, ASI's prayers will finally be answered. We will gladly make adjustments and support their plan and follow their leadership.

According to how America is run and the condition of slave descendants' mentality, ASI already has the only leader in place who is qualified to lead the slave culture at this juncture, simply, because he knows without a doubt that slaves still exist, and he understands the seriousness of the situation. He knows how to get the slave culture up and running as a group. Thus far, seemingly, he's the only leader who possesses these rare attributes. That statement might sound pompous to some, so ASI will explain: Because of the slave mentality that slave descendants inherited, the slave culture absolutely refuses to work together. "African Americans" who think they are already leaders won't carry out orders given to them by what some of them consider a lesser leader, unless they are paid to carry out those orders, and then they won't carry them out properly. It's "a black thing."

With this in mind and ASI having no budget except what our current leader contributes out of his own pocket, another reason why he's the best person for that job: put up or shut up, ASI started the American Slave Movement according to our current leaders' past work record and his approach to doing "tough-minded" business. We defined his duties in such a way that he could fulfill them without help from other more established leaders. Unfortunately, this tactic limits his true abilities and slows down cultural progress, but the job ASI laid out for him to do will get done during his tenure. ASI could do so much more if we could get some help from those "African American" leaders who are already in advancement slots designed to help slave descendants, or if funds wasted on "African American" nonsense could be redirected to American Slaves, Inc.

According to glib double-talk that politicians use to get elected and then *reuse* to stay in office, admittedly ASI's current president is not the best person to lead the Slave Nation in the long run, and he is the first to make that clear. He took over the leadership of American Slaves because apparently no one was at the helm. The political tactics and meaningless double-talk "African American" wannabe leaders have used in the past and are currently using haven't yielded favorable results. The do-nothing attitudes of "African American" leaders simply haven't worked! In fact, ignorant leaders trying to be political like whites and using words they heard white leaders use, while all the time doing nothing, is the very reason why slave descendants are so screwed up. The slave culture needs to be jump-started with truth by the fearless, not lulled into further stagnation with political double-talk by the weak and fearful.

To make sure his approach is different from the approaches that other leaders have tried before, and stays different, ASI's President purposely does not possess a political personality and, at this point, he is not interested in cultivating one. Unlike most politicians, he's a businessman. He usually says what is on his mind if it's good for whatever business deal he is involved in and, this time, the business deal is slavery. He knows that only the truth will help his people. The average politicians think if you want help or support from those who wield power — "suck up!" Even though they know "brown-nosing" hasn't worked in slaves' favor in the past.

"African Americans" who are elected officials prove daily that they are ignorant of racial politics. Trying to make people think they understand cultural affairs, when actually they don't, they wind up taking valuable information in regard to their true culture to the grave with them mimicking white politicians and trying to be politically correct. Leaders must speak the unadulterated truth about slavery while they are alive and have the chance to advocate for their people. They must stop living in fear and deliberately watering down the hard facts of human bondage that are so vitally important to the advancement of their culture. If they have valuable knowledge that will help their people advance, they should share it while they can, before they pass on. Frightened Uncle Tom's taking information to the grave stifles the slave culture from receiving undiluted advancement data.

Slave descendants are far too tenderhearted when it comes to business, and they're too backward when it comes to politics. They must take their cue from America, their mother country, and continually seek stronger leadership at every level — even when they might believe they have the perfect leaders in place already! That's what ASI is already doing.

Flexibility is key — but *not* for me

To successfully run a business, which slavery was, or lead a people, who slave descendants are, it's best not to make enemies. At this point, however, making enemies could wind up being ASI's unspoken job. If current leaders who hold gatekeeper slots won't start leading slave descendants properly, then ASI's main job becomes to expose those who are impostors. Gatekeepers won't appreciate public disclosure and will consider ASI their enemy. "All hell" could very well break loose within the slave culture. Still, we've got a job to do. If ASI doesn't do the job that was laid out for us to do because we fear hurting gatekeepers' feelings — ASI falls short of its goal. Organizations that know which barriers are blocking the slave culture from entering mainstream America have an obligation to tell slave descendants the whole truth, or their officers, white and black, should be stripped of their rank and removed from their leadership positions.

To be a perfunctory bureaucrat or an indifferent functionary in America at large, your best approach is to be well-versed in current topics and be able to articulate double-talk as lip service to improving negative conditions while doing nothing at all that will make things better. This means, in most cases just look good and say what you think 51% of Americans want to hear; keep your head down, your pants up, and stay out of trouble. To be a great leader in corporate America, however, it's a different ball game, altogether: You stand tall, say what you do, and do what you say. Talk is cheap. Political double-talk won't get the job done in commercial America because businesspersons are ultimately judged by the bottom line or deeds they perform that can be measured in dollars and cents. Businesspersons are always held accountable. Accountability is how they get paid, and the lack of it is why they get fired.

Using the 'gift of gab' to move out smartly

Cultural success in America's business arena ultimately depends on an ironclad advancement plan. To sell a racial business plan to America, sanctioning by a diverse body will be required. This simply means that slave descendants must acquire astute leadership that can articulate their needs and explain the benefits of an advancement plan to a diverse body of high-ranking leaders.

Eager to recruit a black leader who might be able to sell a plan who was already in the spotlight and connected to the power structure, ASI considered Dr. Ricky Jones, a University of Louisville professor. His name was at the top of the list because he had been in the news promoting himself as an "African American" leader. Aside from that misconception, which is normal, it appears he shares the same views as ASI: He stated: *"There is no black political leadership in this city."* Comparing his statement to what the other four leaders said who were interviewed by **The Courier-Journal** newspaper, he was the closest to being accurate about black leadership in Louisville, Kentucky. He agreed with what ASI has been screaming from the rooftops; that there wasn't any black leadership in Louisville.

ASI took this into consideration and surmised that Dr. Ricky Jones is a truthful man! Admitting faults denotes intelligence. Since he had stated a bold, coldhearted fact, denouncing black leadership in Louisville *right out in public,* which is not the norm for an "African American" in his position, he was *without-a-doubt* our man! *He has the courage to stand up for the truth!* So, ASI asked Dr. Jones to be the spokesperson for Descendants of American Slaves. Without hesitation, and hopefully without thinking, he told ASI he gets paid to speak. That really surprised ASI's representatives. During our presentation, we told him we were in the process of trying to form the American Slave Nation so *his* people could become a viable entity and be able to seek profitability as an American group. A leader who is a good businessperson knows that getting paid comes *after* profitability!

According to the department he was in, "African American" Studies," our ASI contingent thought for sure he already knew slaves are a destitute people and always have been. ASI was under the impression that all leaders who are descended from slaves would want to step up to the plate and do their part to help slave descendants, their very own culture, obtain true freedom. Isn't that why slaves were freed so they could make it all the way to freedom and not just halfway? Isn't that what Dr. King was struggling for? Wealth awaits all those, white and black, who are willing to join forces with ASI and help lead slave descendants as they chase the American dream. That's what Dr. King was trying to tell us — to join forces and work together, white and black, hand in hand — until *all* slaves make it to freedom!

Dr. Jones obviously misunderstood ASI's intention because, the next few times we tried to make an appointment with him, he was too busy to see us. This is one of the gatekeeper tactics we have been studying. Why should ASI, a corporation that hasn't yet been financed and is only trying to get our foot in the door so we can help slave descendants out of inherited misery, have to pay a slave descendant money we don't have to help his own people — especially when he is already in a comfortable, institutional position and is already being paid to help them? Slaves have "gone through hell" only to find out that it's their own leaders who are hoarding the proverbial pot of gold at the end of the rainbow!

Keep the faith; it's not over yet

As ASI assumes the grueling task of rectifying slavery, we trudge on up the hill taking one step at a time and one day at a time. We say loudly and clearly for all to hear and to those who would try to deter us: We're American Slaves! We've *already* been "through hell!" We might be beat-up and scarred but our sleeves are rolled up and our mind is made up. Our motto is: "When it gets too tough for everyone else — it's getting just about right for us." American Slaves have already proven we can handle it — so bring it on!

ASI has vowed to *never* give up on helping American Slaves make it to true freedom. We make that promise knowing the road ahead will be a rough, uphill climb. So be a little patient with us as we take first things first. Before ASI can proceed further up the hill, we must take time-out and slug it out with gatekeepers who stand guard at the first line of defense in commerce. The battle intensifies as the journey continues. ❖

Greetings from the President of American Slaves, Inc.

I t is a privilege and honor to be elected the first president of American Slaves, Inc. My job entails the proper representation of Descendants of American Slaves. My first task is to construct a foundation on which to build the American Slave culture. The foundation's purpose is to guide Descendants of American Slaves into mainstream America. I eagerly accept this solemn responsibility knowing that if those of my culture who understand America and have learned how to prosper don't team together and look after those among us who are not so fortunate, *we're* the cause of our culture's downfall.

Now that I have the authority to act, I will no longer stand by and see my people, Descendants of American Slaves, continue on as an unenlightened welfare nation while we're languishing right in the middle of America's lavish "melting pot." My goal as the first ASI president is to finish what Benjamin Franklin, so very long ago, Dr. King, now a history book figure, too, and other leaders who wanted to help our people started, but whose goals were unattainable and have thus far proven largely fruitless.

America's Little Black Book explains slavery in a different, more positive light and, consequently, we now have a better understanding of the lack of knowledge that is holding slave descendants back and have devised a strategy that is easily applied and highly practical. Slavery can now be argued in an upbeat, highly productive manner at any venue that will allow the truth to be spoken.

Norris Shelton,
President of American Slaves, Inc.

President's platform and oath of leadership:

I solemnly swear to do all within my power to solidify the union among Descendants of American Slaves, the white culture and other American cultures. I will strive to reconnect Descendants of American Slaves to their established roots and thereby ascertain their true racial identity.

I stand ready to debate the facts of slavery with leaders, black and white, until they understand the seriousness of the lingering, debilitating aftereffects of slavery.

During my term as president, I promise to reintroduce slavery to "African American" churches. I will encourage the debate of slavery aftereffects in colleges and initiate the deliberation of human bondage into the courts of law. I pledge to assemble the best minds available so we can collectively plan Descendants of American Slaves' future while teaching them to do business astutely.

I promise to work toward incorporating slave descendants into the American system legally and do all within my power to lead the American Slave culture into mainstream America with military precision and see that they are properly assimilated — so help me God!

Norris Shelton
President

America's

AUCTION TODAY
- SLAVES
- MULES

Little
Black
Book

By Norris Shelton

Wes Kendall

A discourse about the human beings who were bred in America to be slaves, their abandonment, their continuing lack of leadership, and an investigation into the persistent aftereffects of slavery

Other books by Norris Shelton

◆ ◆ ◆

America's Little Black Book
First printing, April 2005
ISBN - 10: 0-9765417-0-X (hc)
ISBN - 13: 978-0-976541-70-7 (hc)
ISBN – 10: 0-9765417-1-8 (pbk)
ISBN - 13: 978-0-976541-71-4 (pbk)

◆ ◆ ◆

Alley Rat
First printing, July 2007
ISBN - 13: 978-0-9765417-2-1
ISBN - 10: 0-9765417-2-1

◆ ◆ ◆

Crabs in a Barrel
First printing, February 2008
ISBN: 978-0-9765417-4-5

◆ ◆ ◆

Black Name, White Game
First printing, July 2008
ISBN: 978-0-9765417-5-2

◆ ◆ ◆

American Slaves, Inc. Renaissance Plan
First printing, April 2009
ISBN: 978-0-9765417-6-9